THE MOON

Introduction by ISAAC ASIMOV

Revised Edition

THE MOON

by GEORGE GAMOW
Revised by HARRY C. STUBBS

Illustrations by BUNJI TAGAWA
and with photographs

ABELARD-SCHUMAN   London   New York   Toronto

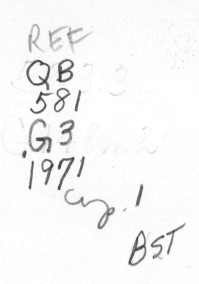
© *Copyright* 1953, 1959 *by George Gamow*
© *Copyright* 1971, *Revised Edition by George Gamow and Harry C. Stubbs*
Library of Congress Catalogue Card Number: 73-137588
ISBN: 0 200 71761 8
Published on the same day in Canada by Abelard-Schuman Canada Limited

LONDON	NEW YORK	TORONTO
Abelard-Schuman	*Abelard-Schuman*	*Abelard-Schuman*
Limited	*Limited*	*Canada Limited*
8 *King St., W C2*	257 *Park Ave. S.,* 10010	228 *Yorkland Blvd.,* 425

An Intext *Publisher*

Printed in the United States of America
Designed by The Etheredges

CONTENTS

PHOTOGRAPHS

ACKNOWLEDGMENTS

The closeup photographs of the moon in Plates II, III, V, VI, and VIII, the view of the lunar far side in Plate VII, and the pictures of the Lunar Module and the Command and Service Modules in Plate X were provided by the National Aeronautics and Space Administration, whose kind permission for their use is gratefully acknowledged.

The quotation appearing on pages 83–84 from the "Strolling Astronomer," the journal of the Association of Lunar and Planetary Observers, by permission of the editor, Walter H. Haas.

INTRODUCTION

The oldest astronomic object in the sky known to man has suddenly become the most exciting. Its motion had already been studied in prehistoric times and its surface had begun to be mapped in detail three hundred years ago. The object is the Moon and it seemed to have reached a dead end as far as human eyes were concerned.

There was no air to obscure the Moon's surface, no bodies of water to mask any part of its solid body. It was a world without change, said the astronomers, and a photograph taken of any part of it through a good telescope would be suitable for uncounted millions of years.

To be sure, only a little over half of its surface could be seen from Earth. The other side was turned away from our planet forever—but that had to be accepted as eternal mystery.

So it was that for a hundred years, virtually no professional astronomer wasted time on the Moon. Its study could be left to amateurs.

And then, in 1957, men broke the shackles of Earth's gravity and sent an artificial satellite into orbit.

The first satellites wheeled about our planet just outside the atmosphere but in 1959, a rocket-powered vehicle was sent past the Moon. Eventually, one was sent around the Moon to take photographs of that hidden side. Satellites carrying equipment of all sorts were put into orbit about the Moon; were sent onto the Moon's surface in a hard landing, but taking pictures all the way; then in a soft landing to take pictures while resting on the Moon's surface and to scoop up quantities of Lunar soil for analysis.

Finally, in 1969, human beings stepped out onto the Moon and human footprints were left in the Lunar surface.

Today, the dead world of no longer ago than 1957 has come to vigorous life. Entire books can now be written on selenography (the detailed description of the Moon's surface) and on selenology (the structure and evolution of the Moon's crust and inner core).

This is not to say that we know all there is to know about the Moon's surface and its structure, however, for we have only really begun to study it. But we have come to know amazingly much, far more than anyone could have dreamed we would a few short years ago.

This book on the Moon was first written in presatellite days. At that time, there seemed every reason to sit back and be comfortably sure that this was one book that would require very little revision. After all, the Moon would always look the same, move the same and be the same.

How mistaken that attitude was! The story of the dead, unchanging world suddenly became out-of-date—not because of anything that happened to the Moon itself, but because restless Man and his endlessly probing, scientific mind carried his spaceships, his instruments and himself outward farther and farther. A dozen years after Man first penetrated beyond Earth's atmosphere, he had lifted himself a quarter of a million miles to the Moon.

Here, then, is an up-to-date version of the presatellite book on the Moon—one that relates all the new findings, right down to the crumbling feel of lunar soil in the scoop controlled by radio impulses from Earth, the crunchy feel of that same soil under the weight of an astronaut's boot, and the alien feel of that same soil brought back to Earth.

Nor will there be any end, now, to these investigations. For Man's exploration will continue and his knowledge on the subject will increase. Eventually, there may well be people living on the Moon, making it a new continent of Earth. And this book will have to be revised again some day . . . and again . . . and again. . . .

ISAAC ASIMOV

1. CHANDRASEKHAR, CARRIER OF THE MOON

When the glorious sun sinks below the horizon and the advancing night sprinkles the dark blue velvet of the sky with myriads of twinkling stars, a divine night watchman begins his appointed rounds high above our heads. His name is Chandrasekhar or "the carrier of the moon," for the moon is nothing but the lantern carried by the watchman. Sometimes he turns the lantern toward the earth and the landscape is brilliantly illuminated by the silvery rays of the full moon. At other times he turns it away from the earth to look at something else and we, the poor inhabitants on the ground, can see merely the thin crescent of the lamp's luminous front.

We are much too prosaic nowadays to believe such legends about divine night watchmen in the sky. Everybody knows that the moon is simply an enormous round rock revolving around the earth and illuminated by the rays of the sun. When the moon is at a point in the sky directly opposite to the position of the sun, its entire face, as seen from the earth, is brightly illuminated and we call it *full moon*. When the moon is between us and the sun, the illuminated side is turned away from us and, for a short period of time, the moon is completely invisible to us. This phase is known as the *new moon*, since a rapidly growing crescent is due to appear right after it. When the new crescent appears, or shortly before the old one disappears, the entire surface of the moon is often faintly visible, illuminated by a dim light. This has been called "the old moon in the new moon's arms." The dim illumination is due to sunlight reflected from the surface of the earth to the moon. It is the equivalent to the illumination of our night landscape by the light of the full moon. Lunar inhabitants, if there were any, would speak of the "earth shine," and would observe the large luminous disc of the "full earth" in their night sky. Between these extreme phases of the new and the full moon, the surface of the moon is visible from the earth as being only partly illuminated by the sun (opposite).

When the crescent is half grown and is on its way to becoming a full moon in a week's time, we speak of the *first quarter*. When it is decreasing and is about to wane into nothing the following week, we speak of the *last quarter*. There is a simple rule as to how to tell at a glance whether we see the first or the last quarter of the moon, but one has to know a bit of French in order to use it. The rule consists of adding a vertical bar to the lunar crescent hanging in the sky. This results in

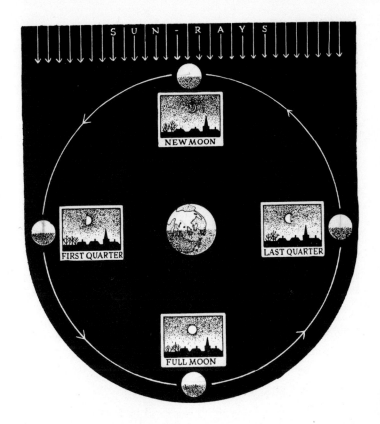

an imaginary letter, which will be either a *p* or a *d*. If we get a *p*, we have the first quarter, and *p* stands for the French word, *première*, meaning *first*. Similarly, the letter *d* stands for the French word, *dernière*, meaning *last*, signifying the last quarter. All you have to do is to remember which French word means what. But be sure to do this in the northern hemisphere only, since in the "upside-down" countries of the southern hemisphere, such as Australia or South America, the rule does not apply and must be reversed.

When the moon is in the first quarter, it is located to the east of the sun and is *following* it in its daily tour across the

FIRST QUARTER

LAST QUARTER

sky which, as everybody knows, is caused by the rotation of our earth around its axis. In this case, the moon rises in the East after sunrise, and is inconspicuous in the bright daylight. But when the sky darkens after sunset, we notice the moon in the West on its way down to the horizon. (Compare top figure.)

When the moon is in the last quarter, it is *preceding* the sun in its daily motion. It rises in the East in the small hours of the morning and remains clearly visible until the sky is brightly illuminated by the rays of the rising sun. (Compare lower figure.)

Revolving around the earth, the moon also turns around its own axis, facing the earth all the time, just like an agile boxer dancing in the ring around his heavier opponent. As we shall see later, this was not always so, and the rotation of the moon around its axis and its revolution around the earth became synchronized only after a very long period. The fact that the moon always presents to us the same hemisphere has led to a number of fantastic speculations as to the properties of its "other side." But that was in the past. No astronomer was at all surprised when photographs taken from both manned and unmanned spacecraft in the 1960's showed this "other side" to look very much like the one we have always known. As a matter of fact, even before that time, we had seen more than one half of the moon's surface. The moon *rotates* at uniform speed on its axis, but the rate along its slightly elongated orbit varies a little. It travels faster when closer to the earth, so rotation and *revolution* do not remain in step. At one time, we see around the east side, at another around the west. Altogether, we can see about 59 per cent of its surface without leaving the earth.

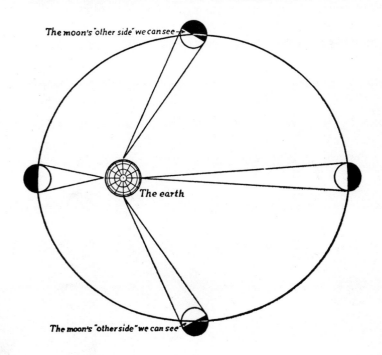

The moon's "other side" we can see

The earth

The moon's "other side" we can see

The phases of the moon repeat periodically every 29½ days (or, more exactly, 29 days, 12 hours, 44 minutes, and 2.78 seconds), a period known as the *synodic month.* Since both the moon and the sun move against the background of the fixed stars (the sun's apparent motion being just the reflection of the earth's revolution around the sun), the length of the synodic month is actually the result of the apparent race of these two celestial bodies across the sky. With respect to the fixed stars, the moon appears to move at the rate of progressing about its full diameter each hour, covering the complete circle in 27⅓ days (or, more exactly, 27 days, 7 hours, 43 minutes, and 11.47 seconds). This period is known as the *sidereal month.* The sun, moving more slowly, makes a complete tour through the stellar sky in a year or 365¼ days* (or more exactly, 365 days, 6 hours, 9 minutes, and 9.5 seconds). The situation is quite similar to the motion of minute and hour hands on the face of a clock.

In this drawing, the minute hand, representing the motion of the moon, is making a complete turn relative to the fixed stars painted on the face of the clock in one sidereal month, or 27⅓ days. The hour hand, representing the sun, moves at about one-twelfth of the moon's rate, completing a full circle

* Since it is inconvenient to count years with a fraction of a day, one extra day (February 29) is added to each fourth, or leap, year.

START   ONE SIDEREAL MONTH   ONE SYNODIC MONTH

in 365¼ days. When, after making a complete revolution, the moon hand comes back to its initial position relative to the stars, the sun hand has moved on a bit, so that it takes some additional time for the moon to catch up with it. It can be calculated that both hands will coincide after a lapse of 29½ days, the synodic month, mentioned above.

If the synodic month were an exact fraction of a year, the phases of the moon would repeat from year to year on the same day of each month, and there would be complete harmony between lunar and calendar months. Unfortunately, it is not so. The year consists of about 12⁷⁄₁₉ lunar months, which advance the lunar phases by eleven days each year. After nineteen years, the accumulated difference amounts to seven complete lunar months, so that the lunar phases again fall on the same dates they did nineteen years before. This nineteen-year period of lunar phases is the basis for the calculation of Easter in the ecclesiastical calendar. Easter Sunday is defined as the first Sunday after the first full moon following the spring equinox, about March 21. Thus, for example, in 1970, the first full moon after the equinox was on March 23, a Monday. The following Sunday was March 29, and this was celebrated as Easter. In 1951, March 23 (still a full moon date) was a Friday, and the next Sunday the 25th. In 1989, March 23 is a Thursday and the next Sunday the 26th. Hence in 1951, Easter was celebrated on March 25, and in 1989 it will be on March 26. Leap years may complicate dates a little; in 1932 full moon was on March 22, not 23.

We are now coming to the important subject of eclipses, *i.e.,* the obscurations of the sun by the moon, and of the moon by the earth. If the plane of the moon's orbit around the earth coincided with the plane of the earth's orbit around the sun

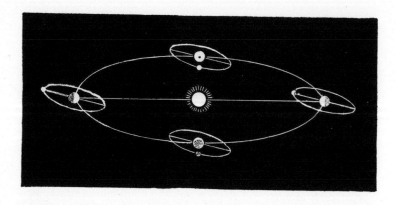

(known as the *ecliptic* because of its relation to the eclipses), the moon would obscure the sun once every month (or, more exactly every 29½ days), and would itself be obscured by the earth at the intermediate dates. However, the planes of the two orbits do not coincide, the moon's orbit being tilted to the earth's orbit by an angle of 5° 8′. As the earth moves around the sun, the plane of the moon's orbit remains approximately parallel to itself in space, as shown above. Twice a year, therefore, the line of intersection between the two planes points toward the sun, so that the sun, the earth, and the moon may be located along a straight line. If this happens, an eclipse will take place, and it will be a solar eclipse if the moon gets between the sun and the earth, and a lunar eclipse if the earth gets between the sun and the moon. In the lower part of the figure, we see the conditions leading to a total lunar eclipse, with the moon completely hidden in the long conical shadow cast by the earth. In the upper part of the same illustration, we see the moon casting the shadow on the surface of the earth, completely obscuring the sun for the population in a certain locality. But while outside the line of intersection of the two orbital planes, the sun, the earth, and the moon cannot possibly be arranged in one straight line, and the shadows will be cast into empty space without producing any eclipse; this is shown at each side of the illustration.

Since eclipses of either the sun or the moon require a double coincidence in the positions of the earth and the moon on their orbits, they happen comparatively rarely. It has been estimated that the *maximum* possible number of eclipses per year is *seven* (five solar and two lunar, or four solar and three lunar), and the *minimum* possible number is *two* (both solar). This does not mean, however, that an observer living in a certain locality on earth will observe eclipses of the sun more often than eclipses of the moon, for when the moon is hidden in the shadow of the earth, it can be seen by everybody on the night side of our globe. On the other hand, the moon's shadow on the surface of the earth is never more than 160 miles across and usually less, so that one must be located in a very narrow band running across the earth's surface in order to be able to observe a particular total solar eclipse. In any given location on the earth, a total solar eclipse happens only once in three and a half centuries. Thus, if one wants to observe this interesting phenomenon, one had better keep the suitcase packed!

As can be seen from the figure on this page, the cross section of the earth's shadow at the distance of the moon is more

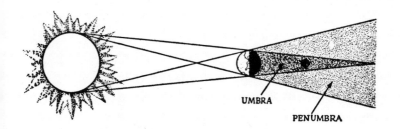

UMBRA

PENUMBRA

TOTAL   ANNULAR   PARTIAL

than twice the moon's diameter, so that it may be completely hidden there for a considerable period of time; a total lunar eclipse may last as long as an hour and forty minutes. But a partial obscuration of the moon can last considerably longer due to the region of the *semishadow* (or *penumbra*), shown above. When the moon passes through the penumbra, only a portion of the sun illuminates its surface and fictitious inhabitants of the moon, or actual human space travellers on the near side of our satellite would report this as a partial eclipse of the sun by the earth. It may be mentioned here that even during a total lunar eclipse the moon still remains visible in the night sky, being illuminated by a dull copper-colored light. This faint illumination is due to the sun's rays being deflected by our atmosphere and thus reaching the moon's surface indirectly. Seen from the moon, the black disc of the earth is surrounded by a reddish-orange ring, the sunlit terrestrial atmosphere.

Turning to the phenomenon of solar eclipses, we must know, first, that due to a cosmic coincidence dating back to the epoch when the solar system was formed, the moon and the sun as seen from the earth have about the same apparent size. Since, however, neither the orbit of the earth nor that of the moon is exactly circular, the distances between these celestial bodies are subject to slight variations, so that sometimes the moon looks slightly larger than the sun, while at other times, and actually more often, the sun looks slightly larger than the moon. In the first case, the sun can be completely covered by the moon's disc, even though for a rather short time, and a *total solar eclipse* is possible (opposite). In the second case, a bright ring of solar surface will be seen around the dark body of the moon, and we observe what is known as *annular solar eclipse* (opposite). Of course, for observers not located in the main track of a solar eclipse, the moon will pass the sun off-center, producing a *partial eclipse*.

How the eclipse will look from any given locality on the surface of the earth depends on the position of the place with respect to the path of the shadow and semishadow. (See below.) In this drawing, the sun and the moon are shown much closer and much smaller than they actually are. Due to the combined rotation of our globe and the motion of the moon,

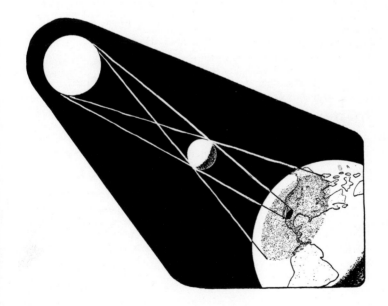

the circles of shadow and semishadow run across the surface of the earth from west to east with a speed of about a thousand miles per hour. The shadow's path, within which the total or partial eclipse can be seen, starts somewhere in the West where the eclipse is observed during sunrise, and proceeds to an extreme eastern location where it is observed at sunset. For scientific observation, the best location is near the middle of the total path of the shadow where the eclipse occurs while the sun is high above the horizon. This pretty well determines the place to which the astronomical expeditions are to be sent.

Until recently, total solar eclipses were the only occasions providing astronomers with an opportunity to observe the phenomena taking place at the edge of the solar atmosphere and in its immediate vicinity. When the bright solar disc was covered by the body of the moon and the sky darkened as if by nightfall, long tongues of flame, known as *prominences,* could be seen rising above the edge, and a faint glow, known as the *corona,* stood out clearly against the darkened sky.

Under ordinary circumstances, when the sky, particularly in the neighborhood of the sun, is brightly illuminated, these faint luminous formations are completely lost against the bright background and cannot be seen. Thus, the observation of these important phenomena, upon which much of our information of the nature of the sun depended, was limited to the small number of total solar eclipses or to about three minutes per year, on the average. No wonder astronomers were traveling to the far corners of the earth, not only for the joy of traveling but also for data of the sun that only the total eclipses could furnish. But, during recent decades, the moon lost its role of exclusive provider of eclipses, when astronomers succeeded in building special telescopes, known as *coronagraphs.* This new instrument simulates a total eclipse of the sun, and, by the use of special light filters, reduces the glare of the sky to such an extent that corona and prominences can be seen and photographed from sunrise to sunset every single day of the year. Interesting and exciting as they are, we cannot go into a further discussion of the solar corona and prominences, since this book is devoted to the moon and not to the sun.

Nowadays, eclipses pass almost unnoticed by the people of the earth, with the possible exception of those living in some dark corners of Africa or other undeveloped countries. This was entirely different in the old days, when the world was ruled by fear and superstition. High priests and court astrologers, of such advanced countries of the past as ancient China and ancient Egypt, taught the people that an evil spirit was attacking the sun or moon and that they would vanish forever from the sky unless special prayers and noisy demonstrations were organized to scare away the devil. This was, of course, pure trickery, designed to maintain the prestige of temple attendants in the eyes of the naïve populace. The perpetrators of this hoax knew very well that eclipses repeat periodically every 18 years and 11½ days (the so-called *Saros* period, discovered by the ancient Chaldeans), and that they would happen again and again no matter what the people did or did not do.

The earliest record of a solar eclipse is found in ancient Chinese manuscripts pertaining to the reign of Chung-k'ang, the fourth emperor of the Hsai dynasty, who lived about forty centuries ago. This eclipse took place on October 22, 2137 B.C., and the two royal astronomers Hsi and Ho were supposed to be prepared in advance to perform the customary rites of beating drums, shooting arrows, and so forth, to scare away the dragon that was devouring the sun. But somehow Hsi and Ho

succeeded in getting beastly drunk hours before the beginning of the eclipse and, when it actually came, they were in no state to carry out the "make-believe" public performance which was part of their duties. Intense confusion resulted and Emperor Chung-k'ang was so irritated about the unreliability of his astrologers that he ordered their heads chopped off.

While the eclipse of 2137 B.C. meant death to the unfortunate and negligent team of Hsi and Ho, the eclipse that took place on May 28, 585 B.C. saved the lives of many Lydian and Median warriors. According to the ancient Greek historian Herodotus, the obscuration of the sun that took place during the fifth year of a ruthless war between these two countries scared both sides so much that peace was concluded. A more recent solar eclipse acting as a dove of peace—the eclipse of June 28, 1451—prevented the outbreak of a war between the Mohawk and Seneca Indians.

But there were shrewder Indians who learned to utilize

solar eclipses for their own personal good. A Shawnee Indian named Ellskwatawa, brother of the famous Chief Tecumseh, decided to use the solar eclipse of the summer of 1806 (about which he had learned from the white settlers) for boosting his fame as a medicine man. He announced to his tribe that he would blacken the face of the sun on a certain date that summer. When the eclipse actually took place, as predicted, his fame among his fellow tribesmen soared sky-high.

In Mark Twain's famous book, *A Connecticut Yankee at King Arthur's Court,* the intruding Yankee, condemned to be burned at noon on June 21, A.D. 528, orders his friend Clarence: "Go back and tell the king that at that hour I will smother the whole world in the dead blackness of midnight; I will blot out the sun, and he shall never shine again; the fruits of the earth shall rot for lack of light and warmth, and the peoples of the earth shall famish and die, to the last man!"

Indeed, strange as it may seem for a man of the Connecticut Yankee's background and education, he happened to remember that "the only total eclipse of the sun in the first half of the sixth century occurred on the 21st of June A.D. 528 and began at 3 minutes after 12 noon," which was exactly the date set for his execution at King Arthur's court. And so, just as the royal magician Merlin approached the pole, to which the Yankee was tied, to apply the torch, the advancing edge of the moon made the first contact with the brilliant disc of the sun. "It grew darker and darker and blacker and blacker. . . . It got to be pitch-dark, at last, and the multitude groaned with horror to feel the cold uncanny night breezes fan through the place and see the stars come out and twinkle in the sky." And when the frightened king ordered the Yankee to be set free, and sent Merlin into exile "the silver rim of the sun pushed itself out

[and], a moment or two later, the assemblage broke loose with a vast shout and came pouring down like a deluge to smother me [the Yankee] with blessings and gratitude." Well, this is as good a description of a total solar eclipse as any!

It is quite possible that this fictional incident was based on an historical event: when during his fourth expedition to the new world, in 1504, Columbus found himself abandoned by most of his crew, and the Indians refused to supply him with badly needed provisions, he relied on a lunar eclipse he knew was due on February 29 to help him. The day before the eclipse, he told the Indian chiefs that the Christian God was angry at the Indians because of their lack of cooperation and that He would punish them with famine and other calamities; that as a sign of His anger He would take away the moon the very next night. When the eclipse actually began, and the poor

Indians became stricken with horror, Columbus announced that they were forgiven and no calamities would befall them if they cooperated in the future. Naturally enough, they did!

Several of these stories indicate that the art of predicting eclipses was developed to a rather high degree in very olden times. With present methods based on *Celestial Mechanics,* a science concerned with mathematical studies of the motion of celestial bodies, one can calculate the dates of eclipses which took place thousands of years ago, and also predict eclipses for thousands of years to come.

A fine example of such calculations is the book, *Canon der Finsternisse,* published in 1887 by the Austrian astronomer Th. Ritter von Oppolzer. This book lists all past solar and lunar eclipses, beginning with 1207 B.C. and all future ones, up to A.D. 2162—altogether about 5,200 lunar and 8,000 solar eclipses. Such exact information on old eclipses is very important for establishing various historical dates which cannot be fixed with certainty from ordinary chronicles. It is known, for example, that a total lunar eclipse took place at the time of the death of the Judean King Herod who, during the last year of his reign, organized the massacre of children in the city of Bethlehem, hoping that the baby Christ would be among them. The only lunar eclipse that fits the facts took place on March 13, 3 B.C., and we are led to conclude that the actual date of the birth of Jesus Christ was four years earlier than our customary calendar indicates. Other examples of historically important eclipses are the eclipse of April 6, 648 B.C., which permits us to fix with certainty the earliest date in Greek chronology, and the eclipse of 911 B.C., which establishes the chronology of ancient Assyria.

2. THE MOON, THE APPLE, AND SIR ISAAC

One beautiful August afternoon during the latter part of the seventeenth century, the famous scientist, Sir Isaac Newton, was sitting in the shadow of a large apple tree which grew in the backyard of his modest home. He was deep in thought, reflecting on the problem of the moon and its motion around the earth.

"Just what," Newton was wondering, "makes the moon go around and around the earth as if it were tied to it by an invisible string. Sure enough, it is no great problem to make a stone, tied to a string, go in a circle; there is the string that

accounts for that. But there is no string connecting the earth and the moon—or is there?"

Suddenly there was a rustle of leaves and a large red apple fell from the tree to the ground. Cascades of thoughts rushed through Newton's mind. "Why did that apple fall? Of course, apples fall all the time, but why do they? Is there a force pulling them to the center of the earth, the same force pulling apples down—in England and in China, in Australia and in Argentina? Don't all apples move toward the center of the earth as far as they can go, no matter where on the earth's surface the tree is located? And could it not be that the same force which pulls apples to the earth also pulls the moon, serving as an invisible string? If so, why not also assume that the motion of the earth itself and that of all the other planets around the sun is due to the same kind of force, originating in the sun?

"Could it not be that such an attracting force is a *universal property of matter*, acting between any two *material bodies*? No, wait a minute. I never saw an apple pulling another apple; there does not seem to be any attractive force between them. But could it not be that the attraction between two apples is simply too weak to be noticed, because *both* are so small? Yes, of course, if one assumes that the force of gravity is proportional to the masses of both material bodies, the apple's pull on another apple must be much, much smaller than the earth's pull on each of them. Sure, one wouldn't be able to notice it!"

And he was completely right. This was the great discovery of universal gravity which, combined with other great achievements in the field of optics and elsewhere, made Newton famous throughout England and immortal in the annals of humanity.

A tale is told that when the episode of Newton's apple became known, one of his neighbors who owned a large orchard met him on the country road.

"Excuse me, sir," said the neighbor, "but is it really true that an apple which fell from a tree in your garden has revolutionized the entire science of astronomy?"

"Quite true," answered Newton, whose brain at that moment was occupied with some other scientific problem.

"Tell me more about it," pleaded the neighbor.

"Certainly," said Newton, who on occasion indulged in good-neighbor policy. "The point is, you see, that in comparing the force acting on the material of the moon with the force acting on an apple, one finds that. . . ."

"No, no!" interrupted the neighbor. "All I wanted to know is how much you charge per bushel for these apples."

The main problem facing Sir Isaac, after the initial realization of the probable existence of the force of universal gravity, was to find ways and means of comparing the force acting on the moon in the sky with the force acting on the apples in his garden. The comparison must have been made on a "per pound" basis, in units of some kind. Using some tricky mathematics, Newton was able to calculate that the pull exerted by the earth on one pound of the moon's material is only $\frac{1}{3600}$ of the pull exerted by the earth on a pound of apples. Apparently the force of universal gravity decreased with distance and, for the purpose of making a numerical comparison, it was necessary to know the relative distances—from the center of the earth—of both the moon and the apples.

As for the apples, the distance is simply the radius of the earth, since the height of the apple tree can safely be neglected. And the distance to the moon had been measured long before Newton by the Greek astronomer Hipparchus, who lived in the second century B.C.

To establish the distance of the moon from the earth, one uses nowadays a method which can be easily understood by looking at the thumb of one's outstretched hand, first with the

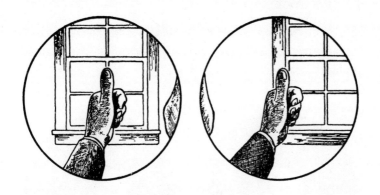

right eye and then with the left (above right). We notice that the thumb will cover up different places of the opposite wall, or, in more highbrow scientific language, will show a *parallactic displacement*. If the object is much farther away than one's thumb—for example, a tree outlined against the background of a distant mountain range—closing one eye at a time would not produce any noticeable effect because the distance between the two eyes is too small. But if we walk a few dozen yards sideways, a parallactic displacement will again become clearly noticeable. In the case of the moon, which is much farther away than any tree, the distance between two such observation points must be at least several hundred miles. If two observers with synchronized watches photograph the moon simultaneously from two distant cities, they will notice that the position of the moon in respect to the background of the fixed stars is slightly different.

If one knows the length of the base, *i.e.,* the distance between the eyes, the two positions of the man looking at a tree, or the two cities from which the moon was observed, and if one also measures the angular displacement of the object against the distant background, it is easy to estimate its distance. It can be done either by calculation using the formulae of trigonometry; or one may do it less accurately by a simple graphical method on a sheet of paper, as shown below.

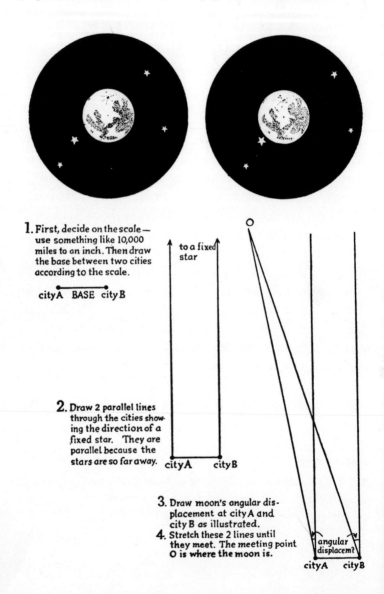

1. First, decide on the scale —
use something like 10,000
miles to an inch. Then draw
the base between two cities
according to the scale.

cityA BASE cityB

to a fixed star

2. Draw 2 parallel lines
through the cities show-
ing the direction of a
fixed star. They are
parallel because the
stars are so far away.

cityA   cityB

O

3. Draw moon's angular displacement at cityA and
cityB as illustrated.

4. Stretch these 2 lines until
they meet. The meeting point
O is where the moon is.

angular
displacem?

cityA   cityB

The precise method, by calculation, yields the result that the distance from the center of the earth to the center of the moon is about 238,857 miles. This is about sixty times the radius of our globe and that is the ratio Sir Isaac was looking for. If the moon is sixty times as far away from the center of the earth as an apple tree on an English country estate, the established value for the attraction of the earth on lunar material made sense. A pound of earth matter at the surface was attracted 3,600 times as strongly as a pound of moon matter— but 3,600 is the square of sixty (sixty multiplied by itself), and the conclusion was that *the forces of universal gravity decrease in inverse proportion to the square of the distance between the two bodies.*

At twice the distance, a given attraction drops to one-fourth of its original value, at three times the distance to one-ninth, ten times as far away results in $\frac{1}{100}$ of the original force, and sixty times away produces $\frac{1}{3600}$.

Newton's idea of universal gravitation revolutionized the science of his time. The mysteries of the motions of the members of our solar system suddenly became crystal clear. Using comparatively simple mathematics—unfortunately still too heavy for the present book—Newton had shown that bodies, attracted to a fixed point by a force varying as the inverse square of the distances, are bound to describe elliptical orbits around that point, which is one of the two focal points of the ellipse. An ellipse is a closed curve, with the characteristic that the sum of the distances from any of its points to the two fixed focal points (or *foci,* singular: *focus*) is always the same. To draw an ellipse, stick two pins into the points which you want to be the foci. Then loop a string around the pins, insert a pencil and draw a closed line, as shown below. If the two pins are placed very close together the figure will resemble a circle; if the pins are comparatively far apart one gets an elongated ellipse.

Half a century before Newton's birth, the celebrated German astronomer Johannes Kepler had shown that the orbits of the planets are ellipses with the sun's center serving as one of the foci, and that the same holds true for the motions of the moon around the earth. But Kepler arrived at that conclusion as the result of purely geometrical studies of the observational material of planetary motion gathered by the Danish astronomer Tycho Brahe. He did not have the slightest idea why the orbits should be ellipses and not some other closed curves, and why the sun should be in one focal point and not in the center of the orbit. Newton's Law of universal gravitation provided the answer to these problems.

It should be noted here that speaking of the planetary and lunar orbits as ellipses does not imply that these ellipses are strongly elongated, as is sometimes shown on some drawings.

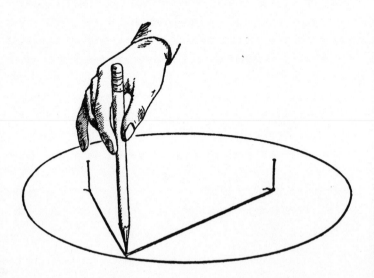

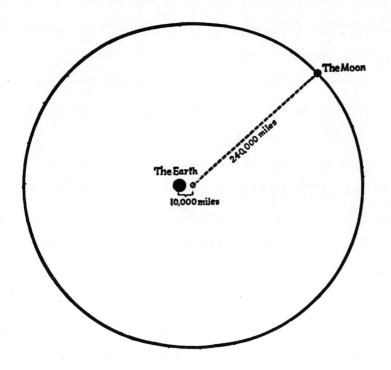

If the orbits were drawn to scale one would hardly be able to see that they are not circles. If the moon's orbit were drawn here large enough to fill a page of this book, the two diameters would differ by less than $\frac{1}{60}$ of an inch. While one focus of the moon's orbit coincides with the center of the earth, the other focus is located about twenty thousand miles above the surface of the earth (above).

As has been mentioned, the forces of universal gravitation are easily noticeable when at least one of the two interacting bodies is very large. Thus, we notice the pull of the earth on any material body located at its surface and it is common knowledge that the tides are mainly due to the pull exerted by

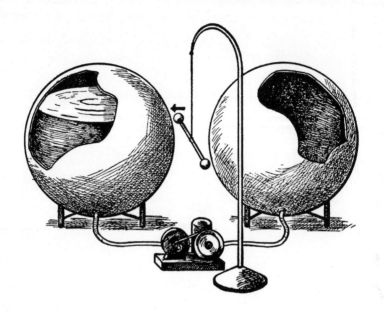

the moon on the waters of the ocean. By using a very sensitive laboratory method, one can even detect the attraction between comparatively small masses. Such laboratory equipment for demonstrating the law of universal gravitation is shown schematically above. It consists, in the main, of two large spherical metal containers, one of them filled with mercury, the other empty. A small electric pump transfers the mercury from one of the containers to the other, and then back again. Two small metal balls are attached to the ends of a long bar hanging by a very thin flexible string in such a manner that one of the two balls is placed between the two mercury containers. When the container at the left is filled with mercury, while the one on the right is empty, the small ball will be pulled to the left by the gravitational force of the mass of mercury. When all the mercury is transferred into the other container, the direction of the pull will be reversed. Carrying out that experiment, one can actually see that the ball moves slightly to the one or the other side when the mercury is pumped. And by measuring the force that produces that slight twisting of the string, one finds it has exactly the value that is to be expected from Newton's Law.

Knowing the distance and the angular diameter of the moon, one can easily calculate its actual size. The diameter of our satellite is only slightly more than a quarter of the earth's diameter (27.3 per cent, to be exact), so that the round-the-world trip on the moon would be only slightly longer than a trip from New York to Honolulu. Thus, the volume of the moon is only about one-fiftieth of that of the earth. If the moon were made of exactly the same material as the earth, it would weigh one-fiftieth of the earth. However, rather cumbersome astronomical measurements, which we cannot describe here, show that the moon actually weighs about one-eightieth as much as the earth. What does this mean?

The answer becomes obvious if one compares astronomically estimated mean densities of the moon and of the earth with the densities of known mineralogical materials. The earth is on the average 5.5 heavier than the same volume of water, whereas for the moon the figure is only 3.3. This is close to the density of ordinary rocks forming the crust of the earth, and we may conclude (as was stated in the very beginning of the book) that the moon is just a giant rocky mountain moving through space. On the other hand, in order to understand the high mean density of the earth, one has to assume that its interior is made of much heavier material than ordinary rocks. Scientists are quite sure now that our earth consists of a dense iron core, possibly in a partly molten state because of high temperatures prevailing in the interior, surrounded by a thick rocky

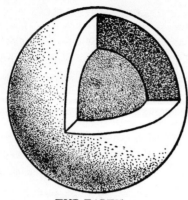

THE EARTH

THE MOON

envelope (above). The belief that the moon does not possess such a heavy iron core, and is made essentially of materials found on or near the surface of the earth, plays an important role in the theories of its origin, which will be discussed in the next chapter.

We have already said before that the phenomenon of oceanic tides is mainly due to the gravitational attraction of the moon. We say "mainly" because the sun also produces a tidal force, which is slightly less than one-half of that due to the moon. Of course, the sun is twenty-six million times more massive than the moon, but it is also much farther away, and, because of the long distance, the sun is weaker than the moon in tide-raising activity. In order to understand how the tides are produced by the gravitational pull of the moon (and partially that of the sun), it is extremely important to remember that the tide-raising force is not the total gravitational pull exerted by the moon on the waters of the moonlit ocean, but the *difference* between that pull and the pull the moon exerts on the waters in the diametrically opposite point of the earth's surface. To understand this better, imagine two men carrying, for some unknown reason, a long inflated rubber balloon (below), one of them pulling in front, and the other pushing from behind. If the "puller" and the "pusher" exert the same force on both ends of the balloon, it will move along without being either stretched or squeezed. But if the man at the front end is stronger or more impatient than the one in the rear and is pulling too much, the balloon will be slightly stretched. If, however, the man in the rear pushes too hard, the balloon will be squeezed.

What does this example contribute to our understanding of the tides? Very much, indeed! The inflated rubber balloon represents the liquid envelope of our globe, the ocean. And the pulling and pushing movers represent the gravitational forces exerted by the moon on the ocean waters on the moonlit and moonless sides of the earth. Of course, there are also the forces acting on the body of the earth itself, and, if desired, they could be incorporated into our analogy by inviting a third worker to carry the middle of the balloon. The point is, however, that since gravitational forces decrease with distance,

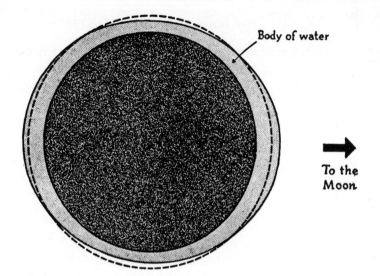

Body of water

To the
Moon

the pull exerted on the moonlit half of the earth will be stronger than the pull on the moonless half. The situation is the same as in the case of the stronger worker in the front and the weaker worker in the rear, when the balloon will be stretched. As the result of the moon's attraction, the waters of the oceans will assume an ellipsoidal shape with two bulges, one under the moon, the other on the opposite side.

The frontal bulge will always point at the moon, but since the earth rotates faster than the moon moves through the sky, two tidal waves will run all around the globe, producing alternating low and high tides every six hours. It must be emphasized that the water does not actually flow around the earth; it is only the shape of the ocean's surface that is changing. It has to be stated, too, that high tide does not reach its maximum exactly when the moon passes through the meridian (right overhead, in tropical regions), since the tides are delayed by an hour or more because of the friction against the ocean bottom, and also because continents are often in the way.

In addition to lunar tides, we have the weaker solar tides. Since the crests of the solar tides obviously point toward the sun, the two phenomena are usually not synchronized. When the moon is either new or full, both the moon and the sun put their forces together and we observe exceptionally high tides. But during the moon's first and last quarter, solar high tides coincide with lunar low tides, and vice versa, so that the total effect is considerably diminished. In the open ocean, where the motion of water is not hindered by the continents, the average height of a tide is about two-and-one-half feet. The rise and fall cannot be detected from shipboard because the ship follows the motion of the water.

The observations were made from isolated islands in the Pacific and other oceans. However, when the advancing tidal bulge approaches the shore line and rolls into shallow waters, its height may rise quite considerably, depending on the shape of the shore line. For example, in the Bay of Fundy, in Nova Scotia, tides rise, on the average, as high as forty feet, and under favorable conditions can reach a seventy-foot mark.

It is interesting to compare the energy involved in tidal motion of ocean waters with other energies observed in the daily life of our planet. Two British scientists, Harold Jeffreys and G. T. Taylor, estimated that the total work done by tides all over the surface of the oceans, like the rolling of pebbles along the beaches and over the ocean floor, damaging the shore itself, warming water slightly through friction, etc., amounts to about two billion horsepower. Large as it may seem, this represents less than one-hundredth of one per cent of the total amount of solar energy that falls on the surface of the earth and is responsible for most of the activity (such as winds, ocean currents, vegetation, etc.) that takes place on it. On the other hand, the work of tides is comparable to the total consumption of energy used for industry, transportation, and other human needs all over the earth. Since tides are mostly due to the moon, we may say that man can match the lunar activity on our globe, but falls miserably short of the activity of the sun. After all, the electric illumination of our cities during the night hours is easily superior to that provided by the full moon; but it is certainly much inferior to daylight.

We cannot end a discussion of tides without mentioning that in addition to the watery ocean tides there are also tides in the solid body of the earth. The earth's crust is not as easily deformed as its liquid envelope; the situation is more comparable to the two movers carrying a piano rather than an inflated balloon. Still, some deformation does take place, and the

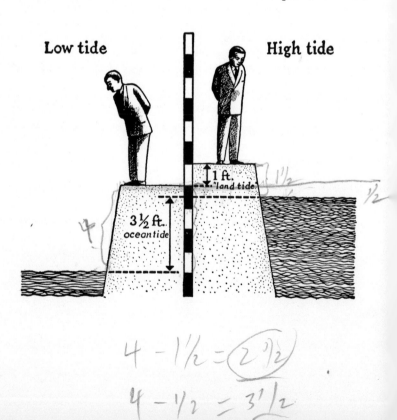

American physicist Michelson was able to find that in the course of each day the solid surface of the earth is twice deformed for a distance slightly larger than one foot. But, of course, we do not feel this daily motion of the ground under our feet, just as the passengers of a ship on the high seas cannot feel the rise and fall of the ocean's surface. The only thing we do observe when standing at the ocean's shore is the *difference* between the rise and fall of water level and the rise and fall of ground level. This situation is illustrated on the opposite page.

water tide — earth tide =

$3 \frac{1}{2} - 1 = 2 \frac{1}{2}$

3. MOON'S BIRTH

The moon moves around the earth with a clocklike regularity; it floated majestically through the sky during the earliest recorded period of human history, just as it does today. But does this statement also hold true if we look back into time millions or even billions of years? Did the moon shine on the giant dinosaurs that roamed the continent hundreds of millions of years before man appeared on the surface of the earth? Was the moon present to cast its rays on the first primitive forms of life struggling for their existence in the oceans a couple of billion years ago?

Strange as it may seem, the answer to these questions can be found in the study of the ocean tides. We have seen that the friction of tidal waves against ocean bottoms and their impact against shore lines dissipate the energy of the rotation of our globe at the rate of about two billion horsepower. We may compare the solid body of the earth rotating within two tidal bulges to the axle of some engine rotating between two brake shoes (below). It is clear that just as the friction against brake shoes slows down the machine, the friction of ocean bottoms against tidal bulges must slow down the rotation of the earth. Comparing the total energy of the rotation of the earth to the rate of energy dissipation caused by tidal friction, one finds that these "cosmic brakes" are not too efficient. The earth slows down at the rate of 0.00000002 seconds per rotation, which means that every new day will be that much longer than the preceding day. This is obviously a very small change, and there

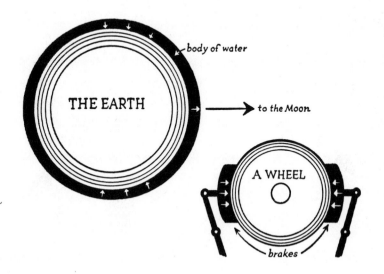

body of water

THE EARTH

to the Moon

A WHEEL

brakes

is no way to measure it from day to day or even from year to year. But the effect accumulates as the centuries pass by. One hundred years contain 36,525 days, so that a century ago days were 0.0007 seconds shorter than now. On the average, between now and then, the length of the day was 0.00035 seconds shorter than it is now, and the total accumulated difference amounts to 36,525 x 0.00035 = 14 seconds.

If this is correct, an astronomical clock synchronized with the daily rotation of our globe must have lost fourteen seconds since the middle of the last century. And a difference of fourteen seconds is large enough to be checked by exact astronomical observations. Indeed, astronomers of today notice that various astronomical events such as eclipses, the motion of planets, etc., seem to run systematically fourteen seconds ahead of the schedule calculated by astronomers of the last century. This discrepancy could also be due to some error in the prediction of various astronomical events, but it is rather unlikely. If your wristwatch says that your train is ten minutes early, it *may* be due to an error of the engineer. But if the television program you wanted to watch also started ten minutes too early, and you find the shop closing when arriving ten minutes before closing time, it is most likely that the world around you runs on schedule and that your wristwatch is ten minutes slow. Thus, the advance in the schedule of various astronomical events is interpreted as being due to the slowing of the astronomical clock, *i.e.,* to the gradual lengthening of the day.

If the tidal forces of the moon have slowed down the rotation of the earth, we should expect that the tidal forces of the earth acting on the moon must have slowed down the axial rotation of the moon. And since the earth is eighty times heavier than the moon, we should expect that the effect on the

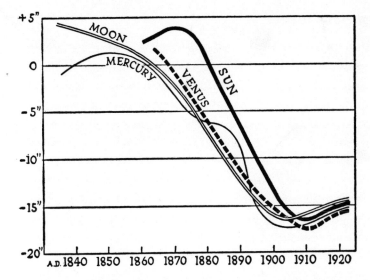

The discrepancy between the calculated and observed positions of the Sun, Moon, Mercury and Venus, in the course of a century. The fact that all curves run essentially parallel proves that discrepancy is not due to some irregularities in the motion of these celestial bodies, but to the gradual slowing of the Earth's rotation around its axis.

moon must have been considerable. True, there is not, and most probably never was, water on the moon, so there could not have been oceanic tides. But, as we saw at the end of the previous chapter, tides are also taking place in the solid or rather semi-molten body of our planet. The fact that the moon is now always facing the earth with the same hemisphere must be ascribed directly to the action of such tides. Now the work of the tides in the body of the moon is done, its axial rotation is slowed down to equal the rate of orbital revolution, and the moon permanently hides one-half of its rocky body.

If the rotation of the earth around its axis gradually slows down, we should expect, on the basis of simple mechanical laws, that the motion of the moon around the earth must accelerate gradually. The situation is somewhat similar to that of the rear wheels of an automobile that are connected by a "differential" in the middle of the axis. When the car makes a turn and the inside wheel is slowed down, the outside wheel is automatically speeded up. The acceleration of the moon causes it to move along an unwinding spiral trajectory, and its distance from the earth is growing larger and larger. Using the figure mentioned in a calculation for the slowing down of the earth's rotation, the increase in the moon's orbital velocity turns out to be such that after one complete turn around the earth, the moon must be further removed by one-tenth of an inch. One-tenth of an inch per month is a very slow rate for the increase of a distance amounting to more than two hundred thousand miles, but here again, we are interested only in the accumulated effect. Dividing the present distance to the moon by the rate of its recession, we find that, three or four billion years from now, the moon will be twice as far away. Conversely, three or four billion years ago, the moon and earth were very close neighbors indeed and could well have been parts of a single celestial body. We could call this hypothetical body from which both earth and moon were formed the *Earoon,* or else the *Moorth,* by combining the beginnings and ends of their present names.

At the time when the moon was so close to the earth, the period of the earth's rotation around its axis (the length of the day) was equal to the period of the moon's revolution in its orbit (*i.e.,* sidereal month)—both equal to what we would call seven hours. At that time, the moon must have been hanging motionless in the sky over a definite locality on the earth's surface; and this is exactly what one would expect if it was

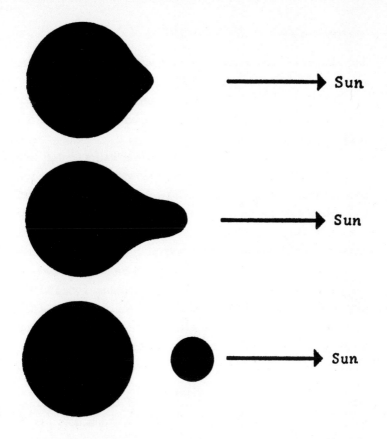

pulled from the body of the earth by some cosmic force. The earth was divided into a "moonless" hemisphere, completely deprived of the privilege of seeing the moon, and a "moon-full" hemisphere in which the moon would have been a giant motionless disc occupying a large portion of the sky. Being so close to the earth, the moon must have been in a semieclipsed state practically all the time, illuminated mostly by sunrays deflected in the terrestrial atmosphere (if any existed at that time). Solar eclipses must have taken place every day (*i.e.,* every seven hours), with the sun hiding behind the moon's disc soon after sunrise, and emerging again only shortly before sunset.

But that was long, long before human beings or, for that matter, any living beings, were present on the surface of our planet!

This concept was first worked out over half a century ago by the British astronomer, Sir George Howard Darwin, the son of the famous biologist Charles Darwin. What Darwin wanted to explain was the origin of the moon, which he took to be literally a child of Mother Earth. The general thought is that, several billion years ago, when, except for a thin rocky crust, the body of Earoon (or Moorth) was still completely molten, a giant tidal bulge was caused by the gravitational forces of the sun. This bulge separated from the surface and assumed the shape of a giant droplet, the future moon. Since the material involved in such a bulge-forming process would consist exclusively of surface layers of the planet, the moon would necessarily consist of lighter rocks, and lack the heavy iron core characteristic of the central region of the earth. And, as we have seen in the preceding chapter, the moon does have a lesser average weight than the earth.

If the moon had formed in this manner, its "birth scar" might still be discernible, and the area of the Pacific Ocean is suspected as representing that part of the earth's surface from which the moon was pulled out several billion years ago! Geologists have found, indeed, that the Pacific basin is characterized by an almost complete absence of granite rocks (typical for the continental massives), and consists mostly of basaltic rocks, usually located much deeper under the surface of the earth. The long and comparatively narrow Atlantic Ocean may be considered a widened crack that appeared in the remaining

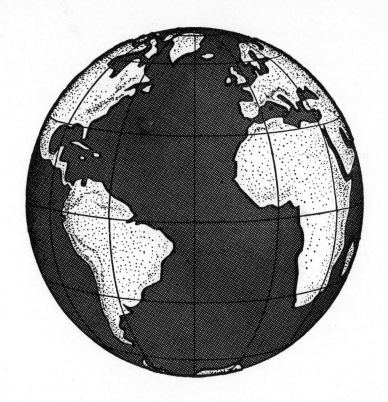

part of the original crust, after a big chunk of it had been removed to make the moon. Such a hypothesis would explain the
similarity between the western and eastern shore lines of the
Atlantic Ocean, which look as if they could be fitted together
like pieces of a torn cardboard.

But, attractive as it is, Sir George Darwin's hypothesis of
the origin of the moon still remains only a hypothesis. Al-
though a considerable amount of work has been done on this
problem, scientists are still unable to figure out just how the
alleged separation of the moon and the earth could have
actually taken place. Many of them doubt outright that Darwin's views correspond to reality, maintaining that the moon

must have been formed independently in the vicinity of the original earth. The problem of the moon's origin is a typical example of how difficult it is to get to know about things that happened so long ago. It is also a possible clue to the origin of the earth; and getting an answer to this problem could give us a much better idea of the possible resources still lying hidden inside our planet, as well as helping satisfy man's great urge to *know*. Many of the experiments which have been set up on the moon's surface, or performed on the material brought back by the early Apollo flights, have been planned with this question in mind; but we cannot expect either an early or an easy answer to it.

4. SELENOGRAPHY

Selenography, composed of the Greek words *selene* for the moon and *graphein,* meaning to write, is the description of the moon just as geography (*gaia,* earth) is the description of the earth. The man in the moon—or, if you are from India, the rabbit in the moon—was the only selenography that was known, until the famous Italian scientist, Galileo Galilei, first turned his crude telescope toward the sky.

Galileo seemed to have heard that a Dutch spectacle-maker, named Jan Lippershey, had mounted lenses in a tube in such a way that they caused distant objects to seem closer. The

mere knowledge that such a device had been made would be enough for any scientist. Galileo, most probably by trial and error, soon had made a working telescope of his own. With it, he became the first man to see the craters and mountains on the moon, the crescent shape shown by Venus, and the strange attachments to Saturn which we know to be its rings (though Galileo could never quite decide what he was seeing here).

To him, the dark parts of the man in the moon looked smooth and featureless, in contrast to the areas where mountains could be seen. He called them seas—*maria* (singular: *mare*) in Latin—and, a little later, as seas they were named by another Italian, Riccioli, when his pupil Grimaldi published a map of the moon in 1651. We still have Mare Tranquillitatis, Mare Imbrium, and so on, though in the last few years we have come to hear their English translations—Sea of Tranquillity, Sea of Showers—instead.

We now know that they are not seas. Larger telescopes show that they are great, fairly level plains with occasional bumps, numerous mountains, many large craters and thousands upon thousands of tiny ones. Each time a newer and larger telescope was turned on the moon, smaller and smaller holes showed up; and when men finally landed there, it was found that these pits ranged all the way down to microscopic size.

There is no evidence at all, even in chemical analysis of rocks which have been brought back by the astronauts, that there is any water worth mentioning on the moon. It is not quite so certain that there never has been, or that there is none *in* the moon, but the chances seem rather small. The "seas," anyway, are dry.

The early telescopes also showed that the moon has no atmosphere. This is not because we couldn't see any air, which is hard to see even under the most favorable conditions. It is because the moon often passes in front of a star while astronomers watch. Then even the thinnest layer of air around the moon would cause the light of such a star to fade gradually— over several seconds at the very least—and probably to change somewhat in color, at the same time. No such effect has ever been seen. The star goes out as the moon covers it, with the suddenness of a light which has been switched off. (Actually, special instruments using photoelectric cells and amplifiers do show a flickering of the light, but this is due to something called *diffraction* [the bending of light waves around obstacles in their path] and not to a lunar atmosphere. Here is one reason why astronomers can't be just astronomers. They must know other sciences, such as physics, as well. Most of our information from space is brought by light, and, if the nature of light is not understood, we may make some pretty silly errors in reading its messages!)

It is true that Apollo 12 set up some "atmosphere" testing equipment on the moon, but this was nothing that a weatherman on Earth could have used. He needs to know about pressure, temperature, humidity and wind velocity. These are things which are noticeable to us near the earth's surface because each cubic foot of air contains about three-quarters of a million million million million molecules (if you like numbers better than words, write a 75 followed by 22 zeroes; but don't expect to picture the quantity any more clearly). These are rushing about, colliding with each other and with us at about a thousand miles an hour. This makes the molecules exert pressure on a barometer and warm up a thermometer and, if enough of them are moving in the same direction at the same time, blow the roof off a house.

Near the moon's surface, a cubic foot of space contains only a few thousand million molecules (perhaps as many as a million- million) and very special equipment would be required to measure their pressure, heating and wind effects.

It is true that a thousand million is a very much larger number than the few thousand molecules which would be found in a cubic foot of space a million miles away from the moon, so, if you want to say that the moon does have a sort of atmosphere, you have some excuse. However, the "air" inside your television tube is many, many times as dense as anything a moon-walking astronaut would have available for breathing, if his space suit were to burst. People have become accustomed to breathing the thin air of the Andes and Himalayas, but no human being could ever keep alive on the "air" of the moon.

Away from the "seas," the moon's surface is a jagged

labyrinth. Some of the features look much like those of Earth; there are mountains and mountain ranges which may be mistaken for those earthly counterparts for which Riccioli named them—Alps, Apennines, Caucasus—if one's geography isn't *too* good. It is not yet possible to say, though, whether the same forces which produced these mountains on the moon operated to make similar ones on Earth.

Other features are strictly moon-type; there is nothing quite like them on Earth. The so-called craters (or cirques, or walled plains, or ringwalls, as they are sometimes called) have few, if any counterparts, on our world. They range from about a hundred and fifty miles across—huge Clavius, in the southern hemisphere—all the way down to microscopic size. Whether they were all formed by the same means, and should all be called by the same class name, is uncertain. Some scientists think so and even believe that the *maria* are still larger examples of the same class. Certainly some of these, like the 700-mile-wide Sea of Showers and the smaller but still impressive Sea of Crises, are nearly circular in shape, like the typical "crater."

Almost certainly, the very tiniest ones were made when small meteoroids struck the moon. These objects would not merely drill holes like a rifle bullet; the lowest speed with which they would strike would be nearly two miles a second, and the *kinetic energy* (the property that lets a speeding car demolish a stone wall) which goes with such a speed is enormous. Turned into heat, as most of it would be, it would suffice to raise the temperature of a stone or even an iron meteorite above its boiling point, so that much of the missile would suddenly turn into a cloud of hot gas and explode. This would blow a hole into the moon much larger than the original projectile. Some of the rocks brought back from the moon show microscopic holes lined with glass. This suggests that whatever made them involved a burst of intense heat which melted some of the stone; and we know that meteoroids range down to grain-of-dust size. The words meteoroid and meteorite are not synonyms; astronomers distinguish very carefully between them. A meteoroid is a small body, generally stone or iron, pursuing its own orbit in space—a sort of junior-sized planet. A meteorite is the same body when it has come to rest on the earth or moon and has become a "geological" specimen. The word *meteor* refers to the streak of light made when a meteoroid is turning its kinetic energy into heat in our upper atmosphere. It is hard to see how there could be meteors on the moon!

The real argument is over the origin of the craters which are large enough to be seen from Earth with a good telescope— say, those half a mile across or larger. One school of thought holds that these, too, are the products of meteorite explosions. The other major belief is one less clearly defined, calling for forces inside the moon, roughly (but certainly not exactly) like volcanic ones, to be responsible. Both ideas present difficulties when it comes to explaining *all* the facts.

For one thing, not all craters are alike. They are all very different from Earth's volcanic craters, which are usually little wider than they are deep; the lunar ringwalls may be so shallow compared with their widths that the mountains which form their rims may actually be hidden below the horizon to a person standing at the crater's center. Of course, since the moon is only a quarter of the earth's diameter, its horizon is much closer; but even so, a crater sixty miles across, with a wall only three miles or so in height, is not very deep. Photographs commonly make them look deeper than they are because the pic-

PLATE IV. *Another picture made from earth with the 36" Lick telescope. The large crater, Archimedes, differs from Tycho in not having a central mountain mass. It lies near the edge of* Mare Imbrium *(Sea of Showers). South is at the top, as in Plate I.* *Note the smoothness of the "sea" bottom, compared to the area around Tycho in Plate II.***

*see p. 65   **see p. 70

tures were made when the sun was low in the lunar sky, casting deceivingly long shadows. This is why Archimedes, the large crater in Plate IV,* looks, at first glance, as though it were perhaps a quarter as deep as it is wide.

Archimedes, you will notice, has no mountain in the center, and this is true of many large craters such as Ptolemaeus, Grimaldi, Plato and Parry. Many others, however, do have mountains or clusters of mountains at their centers; examples are Tycho, Langrenus, Copernicus, and Theophilus (Riccioli, you may have noticed, decided to name the craters after famous people). There is no obvious connection between such things as size or wall height and whether or not there are central mountains, and it is difficult to grasp why a huge, exploding meteorite should sometimes produce a mountain and sometimes not.

You might be tempted to check this theory experimentally by throwing rocks into a sand box and seeing what kind of holes they leave. The idea of experimenting is a good one, but unless you can throw hard enough to destroy the rocks you won't be imitating the meteorite situation very well. It would be better to use something which has no strength to speak of, but which will have at least some tendency to explode. It may surprise you to learn that *dust*—flour, or dry plaster of Paris— will meet these requirements.

Fill a pie plate with one of these powders, and throw or drop a small spoonful of the same material into it from a distance. If you can hit the pie plate at all, you will get a hole *something* like a lunar crater. The dollop of traveling dust has air between its particles; so does the dust in the pan waiting to receive it. This air is compressed during the collision, and promptly expands again like the air trapped in a basketball

*see p. 63

PLATE I. *The full moon photographed through the 36" refractor of Lick Observatory. North is at the bottom because northern-hemisphere astronomers are used to seeing it this way in astronomical telescopes that turn the image upside down.*

when it is being dribbled. This expansion is your "explosion." You can vary things such as the height from which you drop the powder, the amount you drop and the depth of powder in the pie plate. You can wet the powder to form a "mud." All these tricks, and any others you can think of, will change the size and perhaps the shape of the craters you get; some will have central mountains, others will not.

You can even color the dust you drop; a small piece of colored chalk, crushed fine and mixed with the dust in your spoon, will let you see how much of the material thrown around your crater is "meteorite" and how much is "moon." With this trick, you will often find that your craters have patterns of streaks around them, pointing outward from their centers, very similar to the ones you can see on Plate I.*

The crater near the top of this plate, resembling somewhat the navel of an orange, is Tycho. The radiating streaks are called rays, and Tycho has the most impressive ray system on the moon. However, it is not the only one; several similar patterns can be seen in this plate, notably those of Copernicus and Kepler, a little below the middle of the right side (the map of the moon's near side on p. 67 will help identify these).

Experiments of this sort have convinced many people that all the craters on the moon—not just the tiny pits in the rocks brought back by the astronauts—were made by meteoric explosions, but there are reasons to be doubtful of this. We must remember that the air-and-dust mixture is not exactly, nor even nearly, like solid rock in a collision of many miles per second. It is an *analogy,* like comparing a city or a country to a living person. Such an analogy may be helpful, but it can also lead us into bad mistakes—since what is good for a person is not always good for a country. Until we can actually conduct the

*see p. 65

The map of the moon, showing the most important seas, mountains, and craters. The moon is shown upside down as it is always seen through astronomical telescopes.

experiment of hurling mountain-sized rocks at some target with speeds of several miles a second, we can be perfectly sure that any theory we invent will be incomplete if not entirely wrong.

It is not difficult to find facts which the meteoroid theory does not explain. For example, there is the row of craters shown on Plate III.* It is hard to believe that a group of meteoroids was traveling in a line like a stream of machine-gun bullets. Some people have suggested that the pattern was made by a single meteorite bouncing across the face of the moon like a dribbled basketball, but this is even harder to accept.

*see p. 68

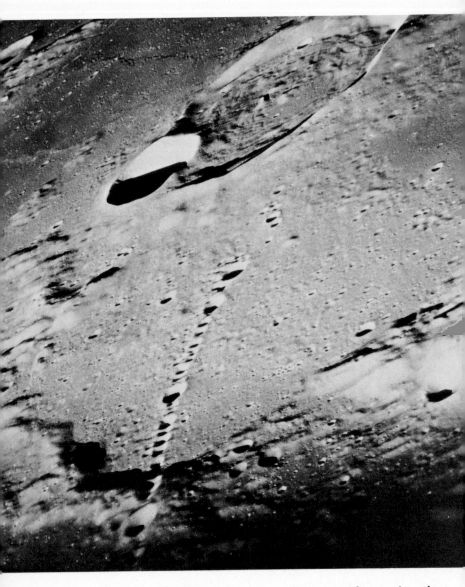

PLATE III. *This chain of craters extending across the moon's surface, near the center of the visible side, is a favorite with people who don't like the meteoroid theory of crater origin. The picture was taken by the Apollo 12 astronauts while orbiting the moon in preparation for landing.*

The large crater in the picture, Davy, is about twenty miles across, and to bounce at all it is obvious that the meteorite would have had to have been traveling much too slowly to explode. Hence, the craters in the row should be dents, not blast pits. It is hard enough to imagine a mountain's bouncing even once without crumbling to bits; twenty bounces are much more than twenty times as unbelievable. Also, the mountain-sized meteorite should still be at the end of the line. It isn't.

The theories which claim that forces inside the moon are responsible for the craters also present elements of doubt. In the first place, the huge ringwalls are certainly not ordinary volcanoes. We have to invent some sort of process which would produce a nearly circular mountain rim with walls steeper inside than outside. This may, but doesn't have to, produce central mountains as well. The process should work anywhere on the moon (there are fewer craters on the *maria,* but they are not really absent there). We may or may not be able to use processes which have happened on Earth, such as the explosion of Krakatoa in 1883 or that of Katmai in 1912. The holes left by these disasters—called *calderas* by geologists—are no-where near the size of Davy, much less of Tycho (Plate II)[*].

When specimens are brought back from the walls, floors and surroundings of a number of lunar craters, we will be able to argue more sensibly about what formed them; but don't expect a sure and perfect answer too soon, even then. Geologists are still disagreeing about the cause and life history of the Grand Canyon!

Another feature on the moon which is hard to explain is the *rille.* Many of these have been seen from Earth and have been mapped quite well with large telescopes. Most of them were assumed to be the same sort of feature as the Rhine

*see p. 70

PLATE II. *The 55-mile-wide crater Tycho, center of the ray system, also shows clearly in Plate I.* *This photograph was made and televised back to earth by the unmanned spacecraft Orbiter V from a*

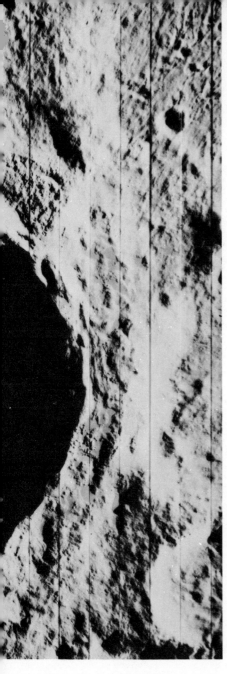

height of 135 miles. In closeup pictures like this, the usual earthly map custom of putting north at the top is followed.

*see p. 65

Valley, which was shaped by the slipping of rocks rather than by water. Such a long, narrow valley is called a *graben* by geologists.

When the unmanned spacecraft, called *Orbiters,* began sending back better moon pictures than our telescopes could give us, it was possible to see that many of the rilles looked more like river beds than grabens. Also many of those which still looked like grabens had snaky, riverlike lines running along their bottoms. Many of the pictures taken from the manned Apollo spacecraft showed the same. Rivers? On the moon?

Scientists have been certain for many, many years that there is no liquid water on the moon. There couldn't be. With no atmosphere—a vacuum—the boiling point of water would be far below the daytime moon temperature, so rivers and lakes would promptly evaporate. The water vapor, whose molecules are much lighter than those of oxygen, would leave the moon even more quickly than the latter gas. Long ago, a well-known astronomer mathematically showed a connection between the weight of the molecules of a gas, the temperature and the so-called *escape velocity* of a planet. This allowed scientists to calculate whether any planet of a certain size, mass and temperature could hold on to an atmosphere of any particular composition. According to this formula, the moon couldn't hold on to anything less dense than sulfur dioxide, whose molecules are twice as heavy as those of oxygen and three and a half times as heavy as those of water.

But the rilles still look like rivers (Plates V, VI)[*] no matter what the formulas say. Some scientists have tried to blame them on clouds of hot, dust-laden gas (which geologists call *nues ardentes*) from volcanoes. Others have suggested that a

*see pp. 74, 76

PLATE VIII. *This picture was taken by the Apollo 12 astronauts while they were walking on the moon's surface, exploring and setting up equipment. This mound would not surprise any geologist if it were found here on earth where rain and similar factors operate, but it is much harder to explain on the moon. The loose rocks show many signs of having been struck, and sometimes turned over, by meteorites.*

PLATE V. *The Valley of the Alps was photographed by Orbiter IV from a height of about 1300 miles. The valley is about 75 miles long. Its walls may have been formed by faulting—the downward*

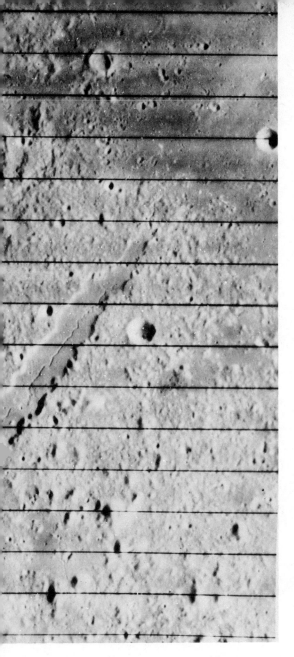

slipping of the rock in the center—but the narrow line down the middle looks suspiciously like a river bed, as do the rilles on both the upper and lower left sides of the picture.

PLATE VI. *A complicated system of rilles near the crater Triesnecker photographed by the Apollo 10 astronauts. Triesnecker is near the center of the moon as seen from earth. The view is to the northwest; the smooth area in the upper right of the picture is part of the Sea of Vapors* (Mare Vaporum).

layer of ice somewhere below the surface was melted by a meteorite impact and formed a mud flow which lasted until all the water boiled away. (This led to arguments about whether ice is strong enough to hold up some of the slopes on the moon—remember how glaciers flow!). One astronomer, however, Dr. Donald H. Menzel of Harvard, just couldn't convince himself that anything but regular rivers could produce such landscape features, and he checked back over the old formulae. To his surprise, and the embarrassment of those who had accepted the formula unquestioningly for so many years, Dr. Menzel found a mathematical error in it; and in redoing the work himself, he decided that the moon could actually have held a fairly dense atmosphere for hundreds of millions and possibly for billions of years.

This changes many of our ideas. Maybe the dark, smooth "seas" really were bodies of water long ago. Maybe rain did fall on lunar slopes, and rivers did wind their way along the valleys; and maybe—just maybe—life of some sort once existed there. Until recently, no one planned to look very hard for fossils in the rocks brought back from the moon. Now, however, anything which looks as though it might be a *sedimentary rock* (that is, one made from material deposited by wind or water) will get a very thorough going-over by the biologists as well as by the chemists and geologists.

Some people, even years ago, did suggest that air and water might have lingered longer on the far side of the moon than on the side we see from here. The idea was that Earth's gravity would have pulled the solid part into a bulge pointing toward us, causing what would amount to a sort of mountain covering half the moon. The far side would therefore be "lower" and might have denser air.

PLATE VII. *The far side of the moon photographed from a height of 1850 miles. While there are a few dark spots, there are no large seas like those on the near side. A valley rather similar to the Valley of the Alps shows near the south edge (at the* bottom *in this view). The small dark patch at the center right has been named for Tsiolkovsky, the Russian rocket pioneer.*

If you read pages 40 to 44 of this book very carefully, you can see what is wrong with this idea. It is the *difference* in gravity between the two sides that is important; the earth would indeed raise a tidal bulge on the moon—but on *both sides,* near and far. Also, the air (if any) and water would be even more affected, forming higher bulges than the solid rock —again, on both sides. There is no reason to expect the far side to be appreciably different from the one we can see from here, and we now know that it isn't (Plate VII)*. Orbiters and Apollos have flown over it, even though no one has landed there yet.

There is *some* difference, of course. If the earth's tidal forces had stopped the spinning of the moon at a moment when the other side was toward us, we wouldn't have a man— or a rabbit—in the moon to tell stories about. The dark *maria,* which are about all we can see without a telescope, are almost totally missing from the other hemisphere, as the plate shows. There are a few small areas darker than the rest of the surface, but none that could be seen from Earth without a telescope. Practically all of the far side is covered with craters, similar to those we have already discussed, and there seems to be no reason at all to suppose that living conditions there are any different from those on the Sea of Tranquillity.

Some people refer to the hidden side of the moon as the "dark" side, but this is wrong. The farther side actually gets more sunlight than the one we see! There are two reasons for this: "Our" side is facing the sun, and having its daytime around the time of full moon (see the left side of the diagram on p. 20). The far side has its day around the time of new moon, on the right side of the same diagram, when the moon is about half a million miles nearer the sun! Of course, half a

*see p. 78

million miles out of ninety-three million isn't a *big* difference, but it is a difference.

Also, the near side loses a few hours of sunlight each year when the earth eclipses the sun—something which never happens on the other hemisphere. If the earth never gets above the horizon, it can't very well cover the sun!

It is tempting to think, now that man has landed on the moon and brought back samples of its material, that there is no longer any point in examining it with telescopes. This is wrong. It is even wrong to suggest that only the huge telescopes of the big observatories can be of further use. Many amateurs have done valuable work with much smaller instruments—often, indeed, with ones made entirely by themselves. It is surprisingly easy to grind and polish the mirror for a six-inch-diameter telescope, and several books are available explaining how to do this. In saying that the task is easy, we don't mean that there is much room for carelessness; actually a very high level of craftsmanship is needed. However, children as young as ten years have made very good telescopes.

The homemade instrument is usually a reflector (see the middle drawing, p. 82) consisting of one *concave* mirror at the bottom of the tube, and a flat one near the top to send the reflected light sideways into the eyepiece. The *refractor* in the drawing at the left is made like the "spyglass" familiar to most people. You can see that instead of only one properly curved glass surface to grind and polish to exact shape, the refractor has four—two sides of each piece on the double front lens. Some amateurs have made such telescopes, but these are apt to be people more interested in the craft of working with glass than in using the telescope when it is finished!

The other kind of reflector, on the right side of the dia-

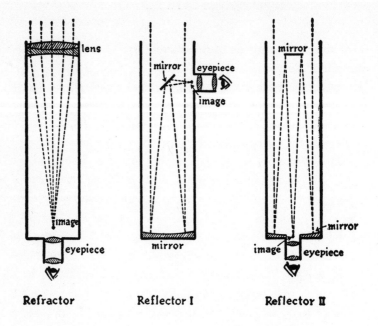

| Refractor | Reflector I | Reflector II |

gram, has a hole in the main mirror which makes it decidedly harder to build—though again, many enthusiastic amateurs have done so.

Generally speaking, the larger the *diameter* of the main lens or mirror, the better the *resolving power* of the telescope— that is, the better able it is to see two close-together stars as two rather than one. However, there is no point in making telescopes too big for moon work; after a while, the blurring caused by the earth's atmosphere makes any further magnifying useless. The thirty-six-inch diameter refractor at Lick Observatory, which made the pictures for Plates I and IV,* is about as big as is useful for this sort of work (opposite). The larger telescopes, such as the two-hundred-inch Hale reflector at Mount Palomar, are used to *detect* very faint stars and galaxies rather than to magnify them greatly.

*see pp. 65, 63

The small telescope of the amateur is still useful for moon and planet study. The Association of Lunar and Planetary Observers says: "Even though Orbiters have produced outstanding views . . . high resolution photography has left many problems unanswered. Such photographs [though highly detailed] represent only a very limited view of an area in space and time. . . . Until the moon is under continual observation from orbit

. . . the role of the amateur will not only remain pertinent but important."

For one thing, there is the question of *changes* on the moon. A feature called Linné was originally reported as a deep crater; it has since been called a "whitish spot" and a mound. Color changes have been reported; so have active volcanoes. None of these are certain, and it is highly important that we keep close watch on our still mysterious neighbor; it is always dangerous to assume that we know it all.

5. MOON PROJECTILE: A DREAM

"During the American War of 1861, a new and influential club was established in the city of Baltimore. . . ." So Jules Verne opens the famous *From the Earth to the Moon,* first published in 1865 and popular enough to have remained in print almost ever since. Verne was not the first to write about a trip to the moon, but he seems to have been the first to base his story on a careful study of the scientific knowledge of his time. He knew the distance to the moon; the fact that for most of the distance there was no air; and understood Newton's laws of gravity and of motion. He calculated, or had calculated for him, the escape velocity of the earth—the seven miles per second which, if nothing interferes, will let an object leave our planet forever.

His Gun Club, after spending the Civil War inventing and building artillery, finds itself bored at the end of hostilities. To keep the group active, its President Barbicane plans to make a gigantic cannon which will hurl a shell to the moon. Verne lived long before telemetry was developed and did not expect the missile to serve any scientific purpose beyond proving that the feat was possible.

A professional enemy of Barbicane's named Nicoll—a forger of armor plate—ridicules the idea, and a series of bets is made between them on the success of the various parts of the project. Then a Frenchman (remember Verne's nationality)

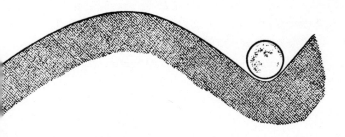

proposes to travel inside the shell,* and eventually Barbicane and Nicoll agree to go with him. The cannon is made, loaded and fired; the projectile is deflected slightly by the gravity of a great meteoroid which forms a "second satellite" of the earth and, instead of striking, the moon swings around it in an orbit which brings it back into Earth's influence. It finally falls into the Pacific and the daring three are rescued.

It has been remarked with surprise recently how closely the concept of Verne's trip corresponded with the actual Apollo 11 mission. Some of this was luck, such as his choosing a three-man crew; but the rest resulted mostly from the fact that the

*see p. 91

basic science needed for the trip was known in Verne's time, and he used it. Earlier writers had less data to go on.

One false picture which plagued these early storytellers (though they didn't know it), and which is still around today, is the notion that the chief problem in space travel is distance. Actually, mere distance in space—while it does have a bearing on the length of time for the journey—is not the real difficulty. A much better picture of a space trip is given here. It portrays the earth at the bottom of a long hill, whose slope becomes less and less steep as we climb it. This steepness represents the strength of the earth's gravity, which does grow weaker and weaker with distance. If the earth were the only object in the universe, the slope would never quite level off. But every other body, including the moon, has its own gravity and is, therefore, at the bottom of its own gravity slope (or gravity *well,* as some scientists think of it).*

The real problem in space travel is to climb this slope far enough to get over the pass between us and the moon's well. After that, we can slide down the other side (taking care, of course, to slow down in some fashion before we hit the bottom). "Escape velocity" is simply the speed needed to keep on forever sliding up the slope of a world's gravity well.

This may sound impossible at first thought, but it isn't—there is no friction in space to help slow down a ship. And, as the steepness of the slope is constantly diminishing it can always, at any distance, be too small to take away the last of our speed.

Since this picture of the problem could not be understood until Sir Isaac Newton worked out the laws of motion and of gravity which we still call by his name, the earliest writers

*see pp. 86, 87

could not possibly have a scientifically accurate foundation for their stories.

For example, in 1656, a Frenchman named Savinien Cyrano de Bergerac (he of the large nose, in Edmond Rostand's play and a Hollywood movie of the same title) published a book called *The Comical History of the States and Empires of the Sun and Moon.* In it, he described a spaceship consisting of a double-walled cylinder with openings at the front and rear. The outer wall contained lenses to concentrate the rays of the sun on the inner one and heat it. Air, heated by contact with this inner wall, was supposed to escape from one end of the tube, driving the vehicle—but not by reaction! Cyrano thought of the air's *dragging* the tube *with* it as it passed through.* Newton—whose third law of motion (action and reaction are equal and opposite) is the real description of the way a rocket works—was a schoolboy when de Bergerac's book appeared, and Cyrano had no chance to learn that bit of physics. Also, the burning glasses would not even have come close to supplying enough power—and, of course, for most of the trip there would have been no air for the hot tube to use.

But some writers were even less credible. Lucian of Samosata, a Greek of the second century A.D., had an ordinary ocean-going ship of his time in his *True History.* To do him credit, he introduces this work with the words, "I write of things which I have neither seen nor suffered nor learned from another, things which are not and never could have been, and therefore my readers should by no means believe them." In another book, Lucian had his hero fly to the moon with borrowed bird wings driven by his own muscles.

Bishop Godwin, in 1638, had a certain Domingo Gon-

*see p. 93

zales carried to the moon in a chair drawn by large birds. Cyrano, in still another story, used an iron vehicle which was driven by throwing large magnets ahead and letting them pull the craft forward (no, Cyrano did *not* have a clear idea of Newton's Third Law!).

But it is the authors of the last half-century who provide the best sport when it comes to looking for really scientific attempts at moon-flight prediction. Just how many such trips have been written up since 1930, or thereabouts, is hard to say (though some science-fiction fans could probably make a close guess). Many of these trips, of course, were not much more sensible than Cyrano's magnets, but others showed a good deal of careful study.

In 1937, for example, in Vic Phillips' story *Once Around the Moon,* the spaceship is a sort of combined rocket and cannon shell. It is launched from a very long tube—much longer than Verne's 900-foot cannon—with the energy coming from volcanic sources. A small lake is drained into a lava pocket; the resulting steam is piped to the bottom of the "gun." This sends the ship into the upper stratosphere, where rockets take over. The originator of the project has earlier gone into a "super-mathematical trance" and calculated how long, and in what directions, the rockets had to burn for each part of the trip. He and his companion circle the moon taking pictures, in perfectly good Apollo 8 style, and return safely to Earth (though ship, pictures and travelers are later destroyed when the disturbed volcano misbehaves). Mr. Phillips has an interesting return mechanism; after slowing down, with rocket power, the ship is lowered to the ground by a large balloon.

There is a great deal of fun to be derived from this sort of story if it is regarded as a game, with the writer and reader on

opposite sides. The writer must make as few scientific errors as possible; the reader must catch as many as he can. Of course, fair play suggests that one should not count score against an author for scientific facts which were not known at the time of writing.

Even with this rule, however, Jules Verne loses a few points. He is correct in saying that there is a spot between Earth and moon where the gravitational pulls of the two bodies are equal and opposite. He describes a fascinating and fairly correct scene in which the three travelers and their dogs are floating weightless in the projectile at this point. However, the fact is that everything in the shell would have been weightless throughout the entire trip, except for one brief moment when they fired rockets in an attempt to change their orbit.

Gravity accelerates different masses at the same rate, as Galileo is supposed to have shown by dropping small and large weights from the Tower of Pisa. The fact that gravity in the story was slowing down an upward flight, rather than speeding up a downward one, makes no difference. The projectile itself and everything within it would be slowing down at the same rate, and the feet of the men would not be pressed against the floor. Verne must have known this, because he was careful to mention that trash thrown *out* of the projectile kept traveling along with it! In other words, this is not something which no one could have found out before actual space travel; it is a bit of applied Newton's Laws.

A similar error was his assumption that the base—the "heavy" end—of the projectile would swing toward the moon when they were near that body and toward the earth when they were on our side of "the line." It is true that there would be a very small tidal force tending to make the long dimension of

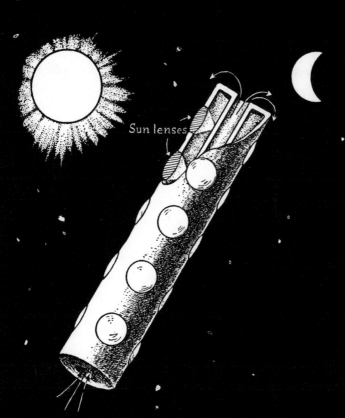

Sun lenses

any object point in the "up-and-down" direction, but it would have taken months for this to be noticeable on Verne's projectile; and the chances would have been about even whether the "top" or the "bottom" would have wound up pointing moonward.

The cannon was also a bad idea, though perhaps Verne should not be blamed for it. Building up the speed of the projectile to escape velocity—seven miles a second in a few hundred feet—would mean an acceleration of about thirty thousand times that produced by ordinary gravity. For most of the trip up the barrel, the shell would have been traveling far faster than sound, so that no rising pressure could go ahead to push air out of its way. Air would have "piled up" in front, like snow before a badly slanted plow. Well before reaching the muzzle, the projectile would have had in front of it a mass of gas nearly as hot and highly compressed as the mass behind it. It would never have reached the necessary seven miles a second. In fact, the only remains of it which would ever have been found would have had to be secured by a chemist sampling smoke from the shot. He might have found traces of aluminum oxide dust (the shell was made of aluminum).

Also, the thirty thousand gravities of acceleration would mean that a 200-pound man inside (or in front, for that matter) would have been pressed against the wall behind him with a force almost equal to the weight of a Saturn V rocket—fueled. The shock-absorbing device described by Verne would have reduced this by something like a thousandth of 1 per cent.

Verne didn't have his crew land on the moon, and didn't try to invent life on the moon. In fact, his three travelers held a formal meeting and decided that the moon was not habitable.

He even made the trip at full moon so that the far side would be dark and spare him the risk of describing it. He did grant his trio a single glimpse, in the light of an exploding meteor, when they saw mountains protruding through a few low clouds; Verne had heard about the theory of air and water migrating to the far side.

But not all the dreams of moon flight were fiction. Men who were experienced mathematicians, competent physicists and good astronomers also gave very serious thought to this journey. Some of them decided that it was impossible—and sometimes they were right. More than a century ago, one man proved that to get a rocket to the moon, the machine at takeoff would have to weigh as much as Mount Everest. His mathematical argument was perfectly right, because he was calculating on the basis of the only rocket fuel he knew—black gunpowder.

At the beginning of the present century, a Russian schoolteacher named Konstantin Edowardovitch Tsiolkovsky showed that a liquid-fueled rocket would travel in space and was a reasonable vehicle for reaching the moon and planets. In the 1920's, really careful mathematical analyses of the problem were made. Hermann Oberth in Germany published *The Rocket into Interplanetary Space,* and immediately afterward Dr. Walter Hohmann put out *The Attainability of the Celestial Bodies.* These were mathematical works, not science-fiction, and it is tempting to think that, if people had paid more attention to them, we might have reached the moon thirty years earlier than we did. The books were perfectly right, after all.

But actually we couldn't have done it much sooner, for reasons to be explained in the next chapter. The dreamers, whether they let their imagination rove to produce entertainment like Verne and Phillips and the other science-fiction writers, or guided them firmly between curbstones of physical knowledge and mathematical reasoning, had to put up with being laughed at. For some reason, it is the thing to do, laugh at dreamers, even the ones who can back their dreams with good, solid, checkable mathematics.

Still, whether they were laughed at, laughed with or taken seriously, the dreamers contributed to the actual flights which have been made to the moon. Without them and the interest they aroused, no one could ever have taken the idea seriously, for there would never have been an idea at all. The dreams gave rise to ideas, and the ideas to arguments, and, as more and more people took sides in the arguments, they brought forth still more ideas to be checked. And, as the checking went on, more and more of the wrong ideas sank out of sight under the weight of the facts.

There are still false notions to get rid of, we must admit; there always will be. But, since we have succeeded in sending ships up the long slope of Earth's gravity well and down that of the moon to a point within two hundred yards of where we wanted, it is safe to say that most of our ideas on this particular problem are about right. We *understand* the problem.

But we understood it long ago. There is a vast difference between understanding a problem and being able to solve it, as a number of people have found out. Many radio lovers, who understand the handbook perfectly and can pass any written test, have trouble building a radio that will work. Many people who understand the comparatively simple scientific laws which explain what holds an airplane up, have never in their lives been able to build a model plane that will fly.

The difference is between *understanding* and *craftsman-*

ship. Scientists understood the basic problem of space flight when Newton published his book in 1687; ever since then, they have had to learn how to make equipment. What this equipment was, and why it took so long to learn to make it, are the questions for the final chapter.

6. MOON ROCKETS: A REALITY

There have been rockets in existence long before the time of Newton, whose Third Law explained why they worked. The Chinese are supposed to have used them first, in the early thirteenth century. But, before the end of that century, they were known to the Arabs and Europeans as very useful weapons for setting on fire towns, ships, and wooden forts. Their military use has varied—sometimes they were dropped in favor of cannons, as when it was a matter of throwing heavy missiles at stone forts, and sometimes they came back into favor when the weight of the cannon was a major problem. The "rocket's red glare" in the American national anthem refers to the war rockets of Colonel William Congreve, a British artillery officer.

These were *solid-fuel* rockets, consisting of a tube containing some variety of gunpowder. They would have worked perfectly well in empty space if they had been powerful enough to get there, but one of the two main factors determining the range of a rocket is its *exhaust velocity*. This is the speed with which the gas from its burning fuel is thrown backward, and it is not hard to see that this speed must depend largely on the energy contained in the fuel. Gunpowder, surprising as this may sound, doesn't have very much energy. Nitroglycerin, TNT, and similar substances are also very poor rocket fuels, though, every now and then, someone who knows very little chemistry suggests using one of them in a space rocket. Actually, a mixture of the gasoline in a car and the right amount of oxygen to burn it will supply much more energy than the same weight of any of these "high" explosives. Chemists now know *why* this is so, and why liquid fuels generally have more energy than solid ones. Since it is also much easier to shut off a liquid-fueled engine once it is started than a solid-fueled one, most of the development work turned rather early to liquid-fuel rockets. (As often happens, we learned more facts later and are now able to do things with the solid rocket which would have greatly surprised an engineer in the 1930's.)

But the liquid-fueled rocket has problems of its own. The other main factor in its effectiveness is *how much* material can be thrown out of the exhaust nozzle in each second. This is common sense; if a 50-pound child dives from the rear of a rowboat he will give the boat a forward kick, but not as much as his 200-pound father will, if he does the same. With liquid fuels, in order to exhaust a large quantity of gas per second, an equally large quantity of liquid must be pumped into the engine each second.

This is the reason—which may be surprising—for the fact that one of the key inventions in the progress of rocket engineering was that of a really powerful fuel pump.

Such pumps are not new, of course. The one in a car forces twenty or thirty pounds of gasoline an hour into the carburetor. In a jet airliner, it will be several thousand pounds per hour. The rocket, however, is in a fuel-hunger class all by itself.

The first really high-performance liquid-fuel rocket was the German V-2 used in World War II. As the diagram shows,

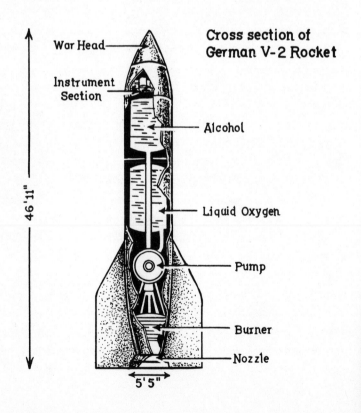

Cross section of German V-2 Rocket

War Head

Instrument Section

Alcohol

Liquid Oxygen

Pump

Burner

Nozzle

46'11"

5'5"

PLATE IX. *Convair's Atlas, an obsolete military missile, is now used to launch spacecraft. It boosted the Mercury into its orbital flights, the Surveyors to the moon, and the Mariners to Mars and Venus.*

this used an alcohol-water solution for fuel, and liquid oxygen to burn it. About 110 pounds of the former and 165 pounds of the latter had to be pumped into the engine *per second,* properly mixed, and burned. The 275 pounds of hot exhaust gas had to be discharged without blowing up or burning up the engine itself. As a side problem, the oxygen had to be kept below its boiling point of 297 degrees below zero Fahrenheit until it was forced into the engine. The pump which handled this task was driven by an engine of almost 700 horsepower— a steam turbine whose steam was made chemically.

The V-2 carried a load of about a ton to a distance of some 200 miles. Its maximum speed was about one mile per second—not nearly enough to send it coasting up the slope of Earth's gravity well for any great distance. It could, however, have served to get a much smaller rocket, weighing the same one ton as the original payload, up to the speed of one mile a second, and the small rocket could be detached and start on its own, taking over from there. If this, in turn, could not have reached escape velocity, it could have carried a still smaller one, and so on. This is the basis for the idea of the *multiple-stage* rocket, which we have used so far for all successful moon flights and which we will have to go on using, until we achieve very much higher exhaust velocities than have been attained so far.

The diagram is not a picture of the Saturn V or of any other particular rocket. It simply shows the general pattern which all such "big boosters" follow. The first stage uses up its fuel getting itself, and the other stages, to the highest speed possible. It is then dropped off, so that the mass of its fuel tanks, engines, pumps and steering equipment will not be a burden on the smaller engines of the remaining stages. The

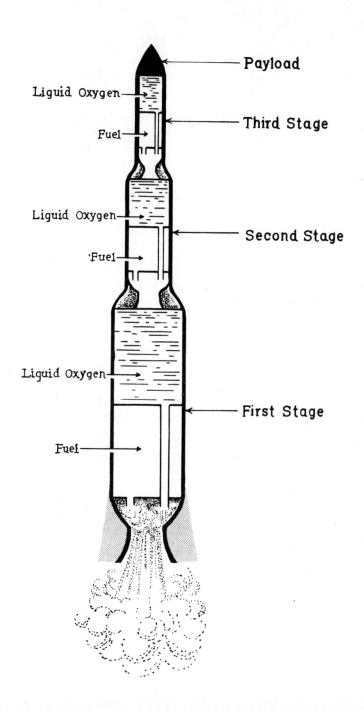

Payload

Liquid Oxygen

Third Stage

Fuel

Liquid Oxygen

Second Stage

Fuel

Liquid Oxygen

First Stage

Fuel

second stage is lighted, boosts the speed still farther and is dropped in its turn, and so on. The weight of the first stage is enormous compared to that of the final load which gets into orbit or lands on the moon.

The actual figures for the Saturn V and the Apollo space-craft it carries will show this: The first stage weighs 4,792,000 pounds, all but 300,000 pounds of it being fuel and oxygen. The second stage weighs 1,037,000 pounds—942,000 pounds of it fuel. These two stages, burning for a total of seven and a half minutes, get the third stage and its load up to *parking orbit* height of a little over a hundred miles but cannot move it quite fast enough to *stay* in the orbit. The 262,000-pound third stage (the SIV-B of the newspaper accounts) uses some of its 228,000 pounds of fuel to add this necessary speed and later gives the Apollo another push up to escape velocity (or, at least, enough velocity to get over the edge of the moon's gravity well).

Then, after having burned for a total of about eight min-utes, the third stage is also separated, leaving the Apollo coast-ing on its way uphill. Since the Apollo itself is still three sep-arate rockets, we may think of a complete moon flight as in-volving a six-stage rocket. The part which returns to the earth weighs about six and a half tons, compared to the three-thou-sand-ton total weight at lift-off.

It seems wasteful. We can only say that it is much less wasteful than trying to do the same job with fewer stages using our present fuels. There just isn't enough energy in chemicals to provide exhaust velocities very much greater than those we have already achieved.

But how about atomic energy? It certainly ought to give us more velocity with less throwaway material. We can't yet

PLATE XA. *The command-and-service modules of Apollo 9 orbit a hundred miles above the cloud-covered Mississippi Valley. Part of the lunar module, from which the picture was taken, shows in the foreground.*

show a diagram of a real atomic rocket; the one here is a "maybe." The problem is that the energy of a nuclear reactor appears as just plain heat. This is nothing but motion of atoms, which is, of course, what we want. If we could transfer this motion from the reactor itself to some other molecules—the lighter the better, since the lightest ones move fastest at any given temperature—we would have a very good rocket indeed. This is what the diagram suggests. A supply of liquid hydrogen (lightest molecule, but boiling point at 422 degrees below zero Fahrenheit) is fed through a nuclear reactor and heated up until its velocity is as high as we want it.

But the engineers have some work to do first. The temperature inside the rocket engines we have is already about as

PLATE XB. *A space-suited crewman of Apollo 12 examines the unmanned Surveyor III that had landed on the moon nearly three years before. The lunar module in which these men were brought to the moon's surface stands in the background.*

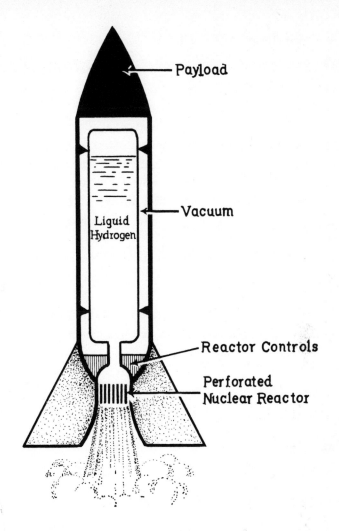

Payload

Vacuum

Liquid
Hydrogen

Reactor Controls

Perforated
Nuclear Reactor

high as we can handle, with all our special alloys and such
devices as using the incoming fuel to cool the engine and keep
it from melting. For heat to flow from reactor to hydrogen, the
reactor must be hotter than we want the gas to be; and at the
moment we don't know of any way to keep the reactor itself
from melting, then boiling, and going out through the ex-

haust—together with the hydrogen and the rest of the rocket's rear.

This does not mean that atomic rockets are impossible. Just as we have had to learn to make special alloys which would withstand high chemical temperatures; to engineer special equipment in order to produce and store liquid oxygen and hydrogen; to invent special tools and devise ways to build the very precise parts of a jet turbine or a rocket fuel pump, so we will have to learn some new arts before we can produce nuclear rockets that will work.

Perhaps we can get around some of the problems with tricks. One inventor has suggested that ordinary atomic bombs, fired one after another, at short distances behind the spaceship, could be used to "kick" it along, as suggested in this picture. It might work, though some other technique would have to be used for the lift-off since firing atomic bombs on the ground is bad. Also this is a very inefficient way to transfer energy to the ship (think of closing a door by swinging your fist at it rather than pushing smoothly with your hand).

One trick, in fact, has led us back to the solid-fueled rocket! One trouble with this was that there was no way to shut off the solid motor once it was lighted; and in guiding a spaceship it is just as bad to have the engine fire too long as not long enough. However, a way to shut off the solid motor has been developed. It consists of blowing open, with explosive charges, a port near the front end of the tube; this does not exactly "blow out" the flame of the burning "powder" grains, but reduces the pressure inside the engine so greatly that it merely smolders instead of burning at full speed. The thrust is ended.

As a result of this development, we now have solid-fuel boosters able to furnish over a million pounds of thrust—not

quite as big as the one and a half million of Saturn V's F-1 engine, but not far behind and a great deal cheaper. A modified version of the Titan rocket, which was used for the Gemini practice space flights, has been equipped with two of these solid-fuel "outboard motors." The resulting triple-barreled booster could put a freight car into orbit, if anyone wanted to.

This all means that we could not have built a working moon ship until very recently. Even though Sir Isaac Newton had solved the main theoretical problem, we did not know

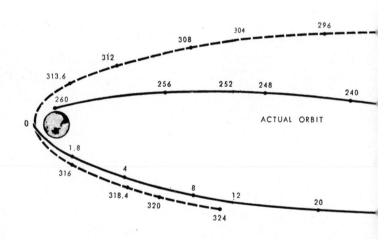

enough chemistry to make adequate fuels; we did not know enough metallurgy to make the light, strong and heat-resistant alloys which are needed; we were not good-enough machinists to make the hundreds of thousands of precise parts quickly and efficiently; and we did not know enough general engineering to make such things as the 60,000-horsepower turbine which drives the Saturn V's fuel pumps. It was art and craftsmanship we lacked, not science.

And if we could have built the ship, we couldn't have

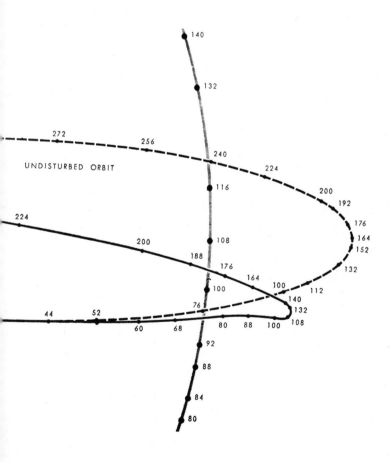

operated it until recently. One other development of the last few years was absolutely essential before we could make a moon trip. This was the high-speed computer. To see why this device is so necessary, look at the orbit diagrams on these and preceding pages.

They are not charts of any mission yet flown; they are meant to show how a comparatively tiny change in orbit near the beginning of such a flight—or better, near a planet on such a flight—can make an enormous difference in the final result.

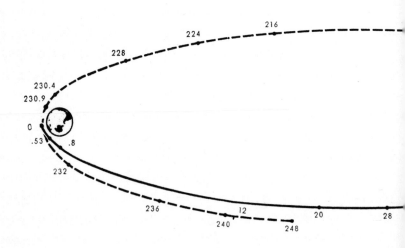

On both diagrams, the numbers represent hours calculated from a starting time when a spacecraft happens to be on a parking orbit rather than on Earth's surface. If you examine the first twenty hours of each one carefully and compare them as exactly as you can—you might even make a tracing of one and lay it on the other—you will find the difference between them to be very small, though not zero. One of the flight paths, however, crosses the moon's orbit at between seventy and eighty hours, when the moon is below (as in the diagram) the

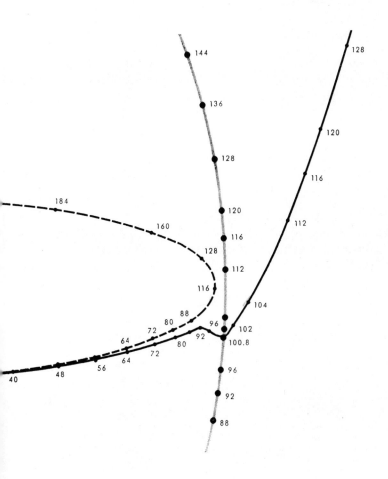

point of crossing. The other path gets to the same place at about a hundred hours, when the moon has already passed this point. In the first case, the ship is somewhat deflected, but does get back near the earth; in the second instance, it heads on out into deep space. Which of these is wanted and which is the catastrophe, of course, depends on the intended mission; the point is that only a few feet per second in speed at the time of original engine-firing can make all this difference.

It is never possible to start a space flight with *exactly* the right speed and direction, except as a matter of luck. We can always expect an error of a foot or two per second; the rockets will have shut down a split second early or late or will have been pointed a fraction of a degree away from the proper direction. This error will be too small to be noticed at first, but will gradually take the ship farther and farther from the planned path. Eventually, this deviation can be measured; and then, and only then, can we start to calculate what correction should be made. This calculation would take weeks with pencil and paper, and many hours with any equipment except the modern electronic computers; these can solve such a problem in a few minutes.

A delay of a few hours in making the correction might not mean much in midflight, when the ship is far from either Earth or the moon (though the longer the delay, the more fuel will be needed for any correction—and fuel is precious). Near any body, however—that is, deep in any gravity well, where the paths of spaceships tend to curve sharply—an hour may be much too long to wait. By the time a correction is made, the ship may have crashed or burned up in the atmosphere.

Strictly speaking, *if* we could afford to be careless with fuel, we could do without high-speed computation. We could keep making rough corrections time and time again, as each new error appeared, like a bicycle rider. However, it will be a long, long time before astronauts will stop watching every drop of their fuel as though it were their own blood!

Now that we have made brief visits to the moon and proven that we *can* get there, the problem of staying long enough to do major study projects has to be faced. As we have seen, there is no air for us to use. There may be water below the surface, but this is yet to be proven. The temperature rises to about the boiling point of water when the sun is overhead, and drops to about 200 degrees below zero Fahrenheit during the two-week-long night *on the surface.*

But the rocks of the moon are excellent insulators; this was known long before we landed there. A few feet below the surface the temperature remains quite steady—somewhat above freezing. The rock above keeps the sun's heat from leaking down during the day, and it would keep heat which originated below the surface from leaking up just as well. Indeed, the moon base suggested in this diagram*would have to have some sort of radiator on the surface to get rid of its waste heat, which would come not only from its atomic power plant but also from the bodies of the people living and working there. However, temperature won't be much of a problem for the moon base.

If large quantities of oxygen are required to refuel visiting spaceships, this could be obtained from the rocks. These consist of silicate minerals not very different (as far as we know at present) from those of the earth; and the typical rock you pick up in the backyard is about fifty per cent oxygen by weight. It takes a great deal of energy to separate oxygen from rocks and it has never been worth the trouble on Earth, except when

*see p. 116

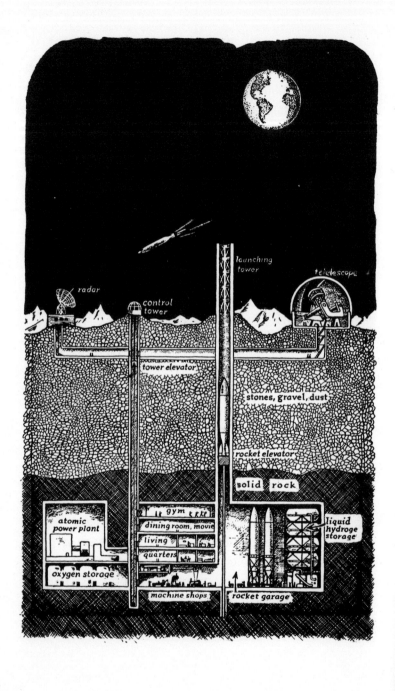

chemists wanted to prove that they could do it; but on the moon this might be worthwhile, and on a large scale it *can* be done if an atomic power plant is established.

Of course, if there turns out to be water beneath the moon's surface, there will be no problem with either oxygen or hydrogen; simple electrolysis will break up the water into these two gases.

Even if there is no water and it proves too hard to get oxygen from the rock, it will still be easy to provide for breathing. The oxygen brought along from Earth will react in men's bodies to form carbon dioxide and water, but this reaction can be reversed by *photosynthesis*. Green plants, provided with light either artificially or through skylights in the upper part of the station during the lunar day, will put the oxygen back into circulation for human use. Such *closed systems* have already been worked. A kitchen garden on the moon would provide its owner with air as well as food.

Once settled on such a base, scientists can explore large areas of the moon either on foot dressed in spacesuits, or in vehicles. They will be able to learn much more, and more quickly, about the moon than we have done so far from the samples brought back. These, after all, represent only a few tiny areas on the moon's surface of over fourteen million square miles. If Martians had landed on the beach at Cape Cod, Massachusetts, and on top of Ship Rock, New Mexico, how much could they learn about Earth from the specimens they might bring back to Mars? (The answer, of course, is: *A great deal* if they were very good scientists, but not nearly as much as if they stayed for a few months or years.)

On the far side of the moon, it will be possible to set up great radio telescopes, free of interference from Earth's broadcasting stations and other electrical devices. With such equipment we could learn more about the distant parts of the universe—including the sun, on which we may have to depend for energy before long. The dry vacuum of the moon may prove such a help in some refining and manufacturing processes that things made there will actually be cheaper than if made on Earth, in spite of the huge cost of transportation (some engineers believe that this will be true; others doubt it seriously). If there proves to be water or some other rocket-fuel source the moon would serve as a much better staging point for trips to the other planets than would the orbital stations now being considered. Otherwise it would not. Nothing is to be gained by climbing down into the moon's gravity well and out again, unless a worthwhile supply of fuel is available at the bottom.

The low gravity may prove helpful to people with weak hearts, or, on the other hand, may prove harmful to everybody in the long run. It will take experience to find out. Either way, we will certainly learn more about biology in general, and human physiology in particular, when men take up lengthy residence on the moon. If permanent living there proves possible, it is likely enough that, eventually, the moon colonies will become self-supporting and perhaps even independent. One can imagine people born and raised there, who would find it impossible to visit Earth because of its terrific gravity, which is six times what they would be accustomed to.

It is fun to guess at what can and will be done as a result of our ability to reach our satellite, but we must remember that we can no more foresee *all* the consequences than the people in fifteenth-century Europe could predict all the results of Columbus' voyages. We can make a few guesses of what *will* result, as we have just been doing. We can have some pretty sound ideas on what will *not* happen, too; for example, it is unlikely that the moon will ever become a source of relief from the overcrowding on Earth. Not only is it so much smaller, but men can live there only under artificial conditions; and most of all, it takes the labor of too many thousands of skilled people down here to lift just three men out of Earth's gravity well.

It is unlikely that the moon will be a source of raw material, except for articles actually manufactured there. At the moment, if there were gold bricks lying around on the lunar surface ready to be picked up, they would not pay their freight charges back to Earth. Undoubtedly in the future, space travel will become easier and, therefore, cheaper. But for a long time yet, the principal return we will get from this effort will be in knowledge.

We can be quite sure that the moon will never be a military station. It has been suggested as a place to hide missile-launching sites, but this seems most unlikely. Aiming would be difficult, though of course not impossible, from that distance, and a missile would be in transit for such a long time that it would be easy to detect and intercept. Since spaceships en route between Earth and moon are easy to detect by radar, it would be very difficult to build and supply such a base secretly. Spying on Earth can be done much more effectively from satellites in orbits much closer to our own planet.

No, the moon barren and lifeless though it now seems to be, with no trace of the sort of loot that lured the Spaniards to America and the Vikings on their piratical voyages of discovery, still offers much good and no obvious harm to mankind. Reaching it is an achievement and evidence of mastery over his physical world, of which man can be properly proud! The knowledge, which is the most obvious reward for that achievement, can only give us a better understanding of our own world and its origin, of our place in the universe and of what we can—and perhaps even what we should—do with our own powers.

Chandrasekhar's lantern is still a guide.

BIBLIOGRAPHY

ALTER, DINSMORE, *Pictorial Guide to the Moon*, Crowell, New York, 1963.

APPEL, BENJAMIN, *The Fantastic Mirror*, Pantheon, New York, 1969.

BEISER, GERMAINE, *The Story of Gravity*, Dutton, New York, 1968.

BERGMANN, PETER G., *The Riddle of Gravitation*, Scribner's, New York, 1968.

CLEMENT, HAL (ed.), *First Flights to the Moon*, Doubleday, New York, 1970.

GREEN, R. L., *Into Other Worlds*, Abelard-Schuman, New York, 1958.

HALACY, D. S., JR., *Colonization of the Moon*, Van Nostrand, New York, 1969.

HOLDER, WILLIAM G., *Saturn V, The Moon Rocket*, Messner, New York, 1969.

MOORE, PATRICK and CATTERMOLE, PETER, *The Craters of the Moon*, Norton, New York, 1967.

MOORE, PATRICK and WILKINS, H. P., *The Moon*, Macmillan, New York.

RUZIC, NEIL P., *The Case for Going to the Moon*, Putnam, New York, 1965.

INDEX